OPERATION RALEIGH

The Start of an Adventure . . .

Sept. 2005

Dear Caroline (and New Moon)

Thank you so much for all of your support for my raleigh adventure ☺

It is very much appreciated and I'm sure my trip will enhance my ability to deal with all of the crazy productions I'm sure New Moon will throw at me in the future ☺

Love from

Sophie

x

By the same author

The Expedition Organisers' Guide
Where the Trails Run Out
In the Steps of Stanley
Expeditions the Experts' Way
A Taste for Adventure
In the Wake of Drake
Operation Drake
Mysteries: Encounters With the Unexplained

OPERATION RALEIGH

The Start
of an Adventure

John Blashford-Snell

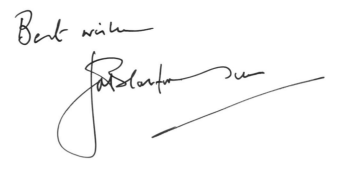

COLLINS
8 Grafton Street, London W1

William Collins Sons and Co. Ltd
London · Glasgow · Sydney · Auckland
Toronto · Johannesburg

Blashford-Snell, John
  Operation Raleigh: the start of an adventure.
  1. Operation Raleigh (*1984–1985*)
  I. Title
  910.4   G420.06/

  ISBN 0 00 217624 6

        First published 1987
        Reprinted 1988

      Copyright © ORPL 1987

Photoset in Monophoto Plantin Light by Ace Filmsetting Limited, Frome, Somerset
            Made and Printed in Great Britain by
        Butler & Tanner Limited, Frome and London

This book is dedicated to
MICHAEL WILLIAMS
who by his courage and determination
has been a sterling example to us all

CONTENTS

ILLUSTRATIONS

OPERATION RALEIGH

Patron : HRH The Prince of Wales

The organisers and publishers wish to extend their grateful thanks
to the following for their support in the production of this book:

Barclays Bank PLC
British Aerospace PLC, Military Aircraft Division, Brough
The Caravan Club
Consolidated Gold Fields PLC
Ernst & Whinney
Mrs I. D. Fraser
Dr Armand Hammer and Occidental Petroleum
IBM United Kingdom Ltd
Kodak Ltd
Lee Cooper Ltd
LEX Group
Mariner Outboards
The Nabisco Group Ltd
Nippondensu
The Northern Rock Building Society
Reed Corrugated Cases, Heavy Duty Products Branch, Langar,
    Nottingham
The Robertson-Ness Trust
The Swiss Bank Corporation
Tate & Lyle PLC
Tea Council
TSB Channel Islands
TSB Trust
The Wig and Pen Club

Operation Raleigh is promoted and organised by the Scientific
Exploration Society.

GUATEMALA
BELIZE
HONDURAS
EL SALVADOR
NICARAGUA
COSTA RICA
PANAMA
COLOMBIA
VENEZUELA
GUYANA
SURINAM
FRENCH GUIANA
ECUADOR
Rio Mayo
Huarez
Puerto Bermudez
Lima
PERU
Tambopata
Machu Picchu
BOLIVIA
La Paz
Amboro National Park
Arica
Chungara
Santa Cruz
Camerones Terrace
Tarapaca
Iquique
Tambilo
Mejillones
Antofagasta
Papaso
BRAZIL
PARAGUAY
ARGENTINA
SOUTH PACIFIC OCEAN
CHILE
Valparaiso
Santiago
SOUTH ATLANTIC OCEAN
Puerto Montt
Chacabuco
Coyhaique
Laguna General Carrera
San Rafael
FALKLAND IS.
N
CAPE HORN
ANDREW WRIGHT

Kaui
Oahu
Molokaii
Honolulu
HAWAII
National Park
Hilo
Volcanoes

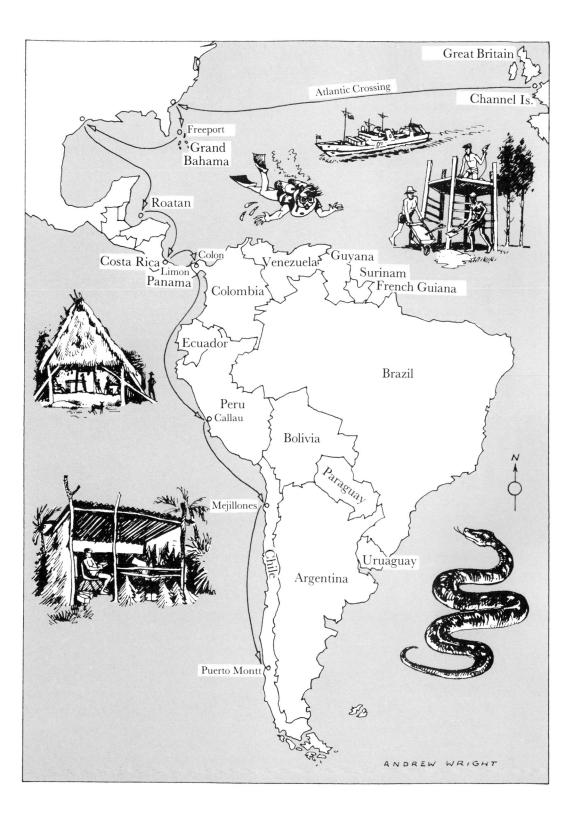

Great Britain

Atlantic Crossing

Channel Is.

Freeport

Grand
Bahama

Roatan

Colon

Costa Rica

Limon

Panama

Venezuela

Guyana

Surinam

French Guiana

Colombia

Ecuador

Brazil

Peru

Callau

Bolivia

Paraguay

Mejillones

Chile

Uruaguay

Argentina

Puerto Montt

N

ANDREW WRIGHT

CHAPTER ONE

In the Wake of Drake

Cathy slashed her razor-sharp machete through the dense vegetation with desperate energy. She had led her patrol over fifty miles in five days, up and down steep slippery banks, through fast-flowing rivers, and always pursued by relentless horseflies as big as beetles. Carrying thirteen days' rations, ropes for river crossings, tools and a .12 bore shotgun, she was humping a hundred pounds and her aching back told even this rugged Scots girl that she'd never carried anything so heavy so far. Originally seven-strong, they'd lost two members within a couple of days of leaving base. The casualties, feet bleeding and swollen from the punishing hike up the bed of the Paulaya river, had been left in an Indian village to recover.

'You're bound to find the city,' the words of the senior archaeologist back at base camp echoed to the machete. 'Just pop along to check it out, shouldn't be difficult.'

After a week of blood, sweat and tears they'd found nothing but humid heat and claustrophobic jungle where everything seemed to bite or sting. Oh yes, Rowland Reeve, their tough American archaeologist and the living image of Indiana Jones, had seen a few signs of what might be an early Panamanian civilisation, but no firm evidence.

Cathy thought all the stones looked natural, perhaps worn to strange shapes by erosion; none appeared particularly unusual. But Rowland was convinced there must be something in this area and so they pressed on, searching for the elusive Lost White City of Honduras. Cathy spat an insect away from her lips, wiped a rivulet of sweat from her face and swung the machete once more.

Clink. A tiny spark lit up the twilight for a fleeting second. Peering into the tangled undergrowth, Cathy realised that the small tree trunk rising from the forest floor was not what it seemed: she'd hit stone. To her amazement she found herself facing a four-foot-high greenish grey pillar. It tapered towards its top: at the base it appeared to be connected to a segment of flat stone. Unlike the tree trunks, the strange object was quite free of any moss or vines. Stepping forward, she felt its cool, smooth surface.

'My God,' she thought, 'it's man-made.'

Her shout brought the others stumbling forward. Rowland was in ecstasy as he knelt to measure the find.

'What the hell is it, then?' Taf Davies flicked a few more bugs from his dark curly hair.

'It's a *metate* – or at least one leg and a portion of the table top,' announced Indiana Jones. 'A form of corn grinder used by the Payan Indians who died out when the Spanish came.'

'Does this mean we've found the lost city?'

'No, not yet, but it's the most significant clue to date.'

So the search went on. More sites were found, stone-faced mounds, triangular and rectangular stones, and implements – an archaeologists' paradise. But rations were running low and the journey back would be no picnic: they had to return now.

Sick with dysentery, their packs seeming no lighter for the reduction in rations, they staggered weakly homeward, the elation of their discoveries forgotten as they trudged through the tunnel of greenery, arched over by tangled, trailing vines. Light was reduced to faint patches of yellow on the leaf-strewn floor; a faint rustle was the only hint of a startled snake slithering aside. Butterflies with iridescent blue wings danced like beautiful mirages in occasional sunbeams. As the stabbing stomach pains increased, crossing even a small ravine became a nightmare for everyone.

All along the route the insects and the heavy, humid heat sapped their energy and patience. The pace got slower and the food got less: Cathy knew they might not reach even the Indian village on what they had left. Roger Wetherby, a young cavalry officer, radioed base to ask for a helicopter rescue, but learning it would take at least a day to arrange they decided to keep going while they could. Now Cathy wondered if they were still on the right track, feeling almost as if she didn't care. Was some ancient curse affecting them? Was this why no one had found the fabled lost city?

'Funny,' she thought, summoning up all her strength to place one foot in front of another, 'to think all this really started four years ago in memory of old Francis Drake, looting the Spanish Main from this very same forest – and now we're commemorating his cousin Raleigh. . . .'

Sir Francis Drake took as his motto *Sic Parvis Magna* (Great Things Have Small Beginnings) and this applied perfectly to the development of Operation Drake. It had all started with the founding of the Scientific Exploration Society (SES) in 1969, when I was an Adventure Training Officer at the Royal Military Academy, Sandhurst.

The British Army is fortunate in having a unique Adventurous Training Scheme which allows its members to take part in challenging, worthwhile expeditions 'on duty', and it was my job to encourage officer cadets to indulge in such ventures for the betterment of their characters and, it was hoped, with the least possible detriment to British international relations!

At Sandhurst I helped to organise up to twenty small expeditions every year: as an engineer officer, I regarded the conquest of natural obstacles as part of my life and heartily enjoyed the job. But as these expeditions became more complex and far-reaching, so the administrative headaches increased. This led to the setting-up of a permanent organisation, quite outside the Army and with charitable status, through which more of such ventures could be planned, equipped, run and, most important of all, financed.

So a group of like-minded colleagues gathered and formulated the basic aims and ideals of the SES. Since then it has become an international body of servicemen, scientists and explorers, with members all over the world, working closely with scientific bodies and with the Explorers' Club in New York, maintaining a network of valuable contacts in all walks of life.

Six years later, in 1975, we started to consider the possibility of linking together what had originally been planned as a series of separate scientific expeditions. All the proposed sites were approachable by sea, which meant that a ship could be used as a floating base, thereby adding a whole new dimension to the exercise while at the same time greatly simplifying the logistical problems of moving personnel, stores and heavy equipment from one location to the next.

The SES has always made a point of including young people in its expeditions, and in 1974 we had been joined on the Zaire River Expedition by three sponsored teenagers, two from my home island of Jersey, and a river runner from Utah, financed by Mr Walter Annenberg, then the American Ambassador in London. This proved such a success that it was enthusiastically agreed that from then on the inclusion of such 'Young Explorers' should become a regular feature of our ventures – not that we ever envisaged taking along quite so many as eventually we did.

But the key factor which gave Operation Drake its unique appeal was the interest of His Royal Highness The Prince of Wales. It had become abundantly clear that many youngsters felt the need to be stretched and challenged more severely than they could ever hope to be in modern society's everyday life. Outward Bound and similar adventure training schemes do their best to provide imaginative outlets for natural aggression and excess energy, but for a lot of young people they do not really go far enough. It was Prince Charles who, in 1976, publicly pinpointed the underlying cause of their frustration and neatly summed it up when he told the House of Lords that what the young were really seeking were 'some of the challenges of war in a peacetime situation'.

The Prince's involvement with Operation Drake dated from 1977 when he agreed to become our Patron. It was not only a very great honour but it also endowed the project with prestige and credibility, which would encourage the sponsors on whose financial backing we were totally dependent. Furthermore, it would help attract young people to take part. Prince Charles is by nature a man of action with a great spirit of adventure who, as he later confessed, would have welcomed the opportunity to join the expedition himself. Although it was understood that his association could not be officially announced until the venture was financially viable and certain to go ahead, he was kind enough to send a discreet message of support in advance. It read as follows:

> Colonel Blashford-Snell has explained to me the purpose behind 'Operation Drake' and I was most interested by its imaginative and adventurous approach. I hope therefore that

it is given every chance to succeed, given all the ghastly problems that exist with raising large sums of money nowadays. From my historical studies I seem to remember Francis Drake managed to elicit some discreet Royal support for his expeditions, but only if the rewards from a little well-planned piracy were forthcoming! Times have changed!

CHARLES

That message, with its characteristic touch of humour, enabled us to take Operation Drake off the drawing board and, with some handsome help from Mr Annenberg, into the realm of reality.

On 13 December 1977, four hundred years to the day after Francis Drake set sail from Plymouth in the *Golden Hind* to circumnavigate the world, Operation Drake was formally launched by the Prince, and the world's press heard the outline of our plans. Unlike Drake, we were only too happy to announce exactly where we were going and what we intended to do.

The venture would be the most ambitious, imaginative and wide-ranging youth expedition of its kind ever mounted. It was to be focused on a two-year round-the-world voyage of the one hundred and fifty ton British brigantine *Eye of the Wind*, captained by Mike Kichenside, which would act as flagship linking four main projects in Panama, Papua New Guinea, Indonesia and Africa. The programme was to be divided into ten separate phases, each lasting between ten and twelve weeks. For every phase there would be a changeover of Young Explorers, all aged from seventeen to twenty-four and carefully selected from countries the world over. They would work alongside seasoned explorers, scientists and other experts on a varied programme of activities aimed at combining the thrill of adventure with the worthwhile achievement of serious scientific exploration, research and community aid projects.

Almost 60,000 young people applied to be part of this unique venture. After a gruelling series of interviews and tests, 414 were selected from 27 different nations; there were also 95 scientists from 29 institutions in 11 countries directing the various projects, all of which brought major successes, not only in completing important research but in providing staff and Young Explorers with demanding, stimulating challenges.

Just some of these exploits make an impressive list: testing live volcanic craters in St Vincent for the imminence of their eruption; searching for and finding the lost city of Acla; constructing for the first time special aerial walkways in the Panamanian jungle, to give scientists an invaluable close-up view of fauna and flora in the normally inaccessible forest canopy; probing beneath shark-infested waters for sunken wrecks and discovering the long-lost Scottish vessel *Olive Branch* that had burned in 1699; a daring first-ever attempt in Papua New Guinea to run the ferocious white-water rapids, and explore the gorges of the Upper Strickland river; discovering a small primitive tribe there who had never seen white men before; preparing a management plan for a new nature reserve in Indonesia, surveyed over some of the toughest terrain found anywhere on earth; rebuilding a three-hundred-foot bridge at a lodge in Kenya's Aberdare mountains; and a successful pollution monitoring experiment working with the United Nations Environmental Programme, using *Eye of the Wind* and the Goodyear airship *Europa*.

It all ended with the triumphant return of the flagship to London on 13 December 1980. Thanks to the efforts of an energetic PR team, massive publicity had surrounded the venture from start to finish. The press had been both sympathetic and helpful. British independent radio stations, led by London's Capital Radio, played a major role in publicising this slightly crazy scheme that seemed to work so well and produced a steady flow of exciting tales. Finally, there was a splendid TV documentary.

In 1977, and in 1978 at the start of the voyage, we never appreciated just how much bigger and better the whole venture would become once it got under way and international interest grew. In fact, we nearly doubled our original target of 216 Young Explorers, and the total number of people involved as administrators, scientists, engineers, communications experts and fund raisers, plus countless others who played unofficial but often vital roles behind the scenes, rose to well over 2000. The cost in hard cash – not counting the incalculable thousands of pounds' worth of free and cut-price travel facilities, goods and services donated by friends and supporters in commerce and industry – rose from an early estimate of £650,000 to over £900,000.

In November 1979 my Tactical Headquarters, which controlled the expedition, was based at Lae in Papua New Guinea. The rain had stopped but the heavy night air was no cooler as I walked up the steps of the wooden chalet that housed our office. Bent over the radio, the operator was scribbling down messages crackling through from England. As I entered he looked up: 'George Thurston's on, says he'd like to speak to you . . .'

Slipping on the earphones, I took the mike and heard George's distant voice. Never a man to waste words, he came straight to the point.

'I had breakfast with our Patron this morning.'

'Good Lord,' I said, 'have we done something terrible?'

'Far from it. The Prince is rather pleased with progress and thinks we should do it all again – on a bigger scale.'

I took a deep breath and sat down. Later that night, out on the verandah at the home of my old schoolfriend, Nigel Porteous, I told him of the radio message. Pouring me a large scotch, he said: 'Well, you'll need a bigger, faster ship,' and I listened intently whilst Nigel, himself a master mariner, put forward his ideas for a larger scale operation with a motor vessel as flagship.

At this halfway stage Operation Drake's finances were anything but healthy; in fact our committee in London were growing daily more concerned about our solvency. Our Chairman, General Sir John Mogg, had recently met Prince Charles at Badminton.

'How's it going?' enquired the Prince.

'Will I end up in the Tower of London if we go into the red, sir?' responded the General.

'Oh no,' said our Patron, 'you'll probably go to Caernarvon Castle – that's mine and far worse.'

So I wondered if this really was the time to start planning an even grander enterprise. Still, feeling it might help to take my mind off present problems, I opened a file, and marked it 'Operation Drake 2'.

CHAPTER TWO

Mud, Sweat and Tears

Operation Drake had ended in a flourish of glory and over two hundred of the young people who had taken part had somehow made their way to London to welcome their flagship as she sailed majestically up the Thames. *Eye of the Wind* was joined with split-second timing as she passed beneath Tower Bridge by the Beaver of the Army Air Corps that had supported us in Kenya, and a C130 Hercules of the RAF.

The weather was grey and chilly but an enormous crowd had packed the Embankment and the bridge approaches. I shall never forget the cheering, the ships' sirens, the hooting of tug horns. I wondered what the *Golden Hind*'s reception had been like when she returned to the Thames in 1581.

Prince Charles met the young people and visited the exhibitions set up around St Katherine's Dock. For the rest of us, a week of partying and meetings followed, and then it was time to get down to serious planning for Operation Drake's follow-up venture.

The Operation Drake Fellowship was formed to support former Young Explorers in their future projects, but we very quickly realised that providing some possible solutions to the growing problems of underprivileged young people in Britain should be high on our agenda.

Those of us who had spent many hours talking with inner city youngsters knew how easy it was for some relatively minor incident to trigger off violence. As if to prove the point, Britain was suddenly swept by the worst youth riots ever known here; the average law-abiding citizen could not believe that this sort of thing was actually happening in their own country. I could remember visiting a youth club in south London and meeting face-to-face bored, frustrated and restless young people who found it difficult even to talk to someone they thought might be a member of the Establishment.

'Is you the fuzz?' spat one of them, reeking of pot, glaring at me from bloodshot eyes only a few inches away.

'No,' I replied, 'I'm a soldier.'

'What do you do then?' he snarled, but before I could reply, one of the club organisers, another young coloured boy, said: 'You know, man – he kills people.'

The face in front of me unexpectedly broke into a smile. 'Violence rules okay.' I was invited for a drink: but not before I had seen the fearful hatred pent up inside him.

The majority of the people of Britain who had not wanted to witness the riots of 1981 could turn to another TV channel, but having seen the trouble spots at close hand I feared the day might come when viewers' interest would be forced – the violence would be at their own front doors. Many who'd worked tirelessly on Operation Drake saw that we must do something quickly to help this mass of rebellious youth that was gaining more and more confidence in its own violent potential, so we converted the aim of the Operation Drake Fellowship into one of assisting disadvantaged youngsters in Britain, in the hope that we were not too late. The Drake Fellowship, as it is now known, has grown in size and stature thanks to considerable help from many of the individuals and companies who were involved with our first round-the-world expedition.

During Operation Drake we'd found that the young had wanted much more responsibility; therefore, the new expedition should be designed to include tasks to suit this need. We had learned the value of young leaders and were convinced that they had a better chance of communicating with other young people, of inspiring them with the same pioneer spirit, than leaders of my generation. We had come to feel, too, that the more youngsters who could share in an experience like Drake, the better the world's future would be; so we decided that for the next venture we would increase the number of countries taking part to well over 50, and the number of participants to 4000. We didn't foresee any difficulty about reaching that target worldwide, but there still remained the problem of finding quite large numbers of suitable young leaders.

It was early in 1982 when I first heard the suggestion that the Armed Forces should take large numbers of young people, especially from the inner cities, and give them adventurous, character-building training in the great outdoors. I was not confident that my military colleagues would be greatly sympathetic to the needs of the sort of teenagers I had met, so I was not over-pleased to be given command of the Army's part in this new enterprise. Nevertheless, I was determined to make the best of what seemed to be an impossible task to achieve in one year, and so the Fort George Volunteers were created.

Based at the massive fortress near Inverness in the Highlands of Scotland after which it was named, the aim was to take some 2500 restless, frustrated and largely unemployed teenagers from all walks of life and teach them some self-reliance and self-respect. Although I was given every support by the Government and the Armed Forces, I do not now believe we could have achieved so much without the friendly cooperation of the people of Scotland and the assistance of many who had helped on previous Drake expeditions.

To my surprise the scheme was a success, and I learnt much about the needs of modern youth. I saw that the longer people were unemployed, the longer they were likely to remain unemployed. It was a frightening statistic during my time in Inverness that, in 1983, there were over 7.5 million British young people between seventeen and twenty-four and of these, some 1.2 million were unemployed. Not only did they lack jobs, they lacked any direction to their lives and, it seemed, any will to find one. Is this, I asked myself, a product of the swinging sixties? For that was a decade when old values were being questioned, youngsters were reared with family ties a little looser and parental discipline slacker. Perhaps the sixties had swung too far. At Fort George the young showed they wanted challenges and inspiration, and during each group's two-week stay at that bleak establishment I saw a great change in them.

In the middle of 1983, after the enterprise had ended, I was asked to find a number of ex-Fort George volunteers to be interviewed by the London press; amazingly, I couldn't find any in London who were still unemployed. Eventually a few took time off work to be interviewed, and one point was made by nearly all of them: they said they'd got jobs because of the self-confidence gained at Fort George.

Drake, Sir Walter Raleigh's cousin, had been a fiercely nationalistic privateer. Raleigh was more of an internationalist, trying to settle a society in a New World and build something lasting. It was felt that the new expedition should be named after him and that it should set out in 1984, the 400th anniversary of the founding of English-speaking America in what is now North Carolina. Prince Charles had liked the name, so Operation Raleigh it was, and with the Prince as Patron the new and greater machine ground into action.

Our aim was to develop leadership potential in young people through the medium of expeditions, using, as far as possible, the lessons learned from Fort George and Operation Drake. On Drake there was no doubt that the administration could have been made simpler. To move large quantities of stores into remote areas had been immensely expensive, so in the future we intended to have a large number of 'backpack' teams who would simply carry their basic needs in rucksacks, and improve local economies in a small way by buying food on the spot.

Each Venturer, as they came to be called, would spend approximately three months in the field. It was not difficult to decide on a route. Weather charts dictated we should 'go west' and an invitation from Jack Hayward to visit the Bahamas as our first port of call proved irresistible. We would go to America first, to the site where Raleigh's colonists had landed. Then it would be south to the Caribbean, Central and South America and across the Pacific to Australasia; perhaps we might even get to Antarctica. The scientists were fascinated by Indonesia and wanted to return there; we also wanted to break new ground in Japan and Tibet. There were interesting possibilities in Pakistan and from my own experiences in Oman I knew there would be worthwhile tasks in its challenging desert. Africa, of course, could not be missed from the route of any worldwide expedition, and after that we planned to return to South America before going back to Britain in 1988 via the wastes of Arctic Canada.

Though *Eye of the Wind* had carried out important marine biological studies during the long sea passages, Nigel Porteous was right; she would be too small and too slow to give much real support to the land operations to come. Nevertheless, manning a sailing ship had provided much of the fun and a lot of the challenges to Operation Drake's young people, so we were determined to find one for Operation Raleigh, as well as a larger, engine-driven flagship.

Before we could do anything we required some hefty finance and we were indeed fortunate that our good friend Walter Annenberg once

27

again stepped into the breach and provided the necessary seed money. The next essential items were a dedicated, hard-working staff who would not expect any remuneration, and a team of enthusiastic experts to advise us on the setting-up of what would become a multi-million-pound venture.

Luckily I met a charming and enthusiastic businessman at a luncheon in London, David King. At that time deputy chairman of a large insurance company, David had been a soldier, policeman and publican but freely admitted that what he liked best was working with young people. I invited him to join Operation Raleigh to direct business affairs and a good choice he was for he brought with him, and helped to recruit, an outstandingly talented team. There can never be room in a book this size to acknowledge all the 'backroom' men and women who have helped to make Operation Raleigh a success. They have to deal with everything from legal problems to scientific programming and on-the-spot leadership, from selection of the Venturers to providing good, non-stop publicity. Some of them will appear in these pages as the story unfolds; others are gratefully acknowledged at the end of the book.

There were quite a few local difficulties in approaching the proposed host countries for the various projects. All the liaison and reconnaissance teams who toured the world did sterling work but I found that in dealing with the US in particular, the greatest difficulty was getting the inhabitants of one state to co-operate with those of another.

I made many visits to Texas where Prince Charles during his stay had played polo and sown the first seeds of the idea for Operation Raleigh. The Texans were highly independent but most hospitable, and on one trip I arrived to be given complimentary accommodation in a luxury downtown hotel. It was late, I was tired, the thought of dinner with twenty or thirty guests was distracting, so, as I was ushered to my penthouse suite by the proud manager, it was not easy to demonstrate an appropriate amount of enthusiasm as he rushed about singing the praises of the hi-fi, the TV, the fridge full of champagne, the four-poster bed and other accessories that added up to a bill, had I been paying it, of $400 per night. Finally came the tour of the bathroom, by which time I was barely awake. The taps were golden and there was even a golden razor; there were separate bath and shower rooms and, as far as I could judge, several different types of loo; the only device that really intrigued me appeared to be called the 'gazooza'. With a final flourish of explanation the manager, realising how exhausted his guest must be, backed out, smiling. I was left with the four-poster bed, the champagne, the fruit and the 'gazooza'.

By now cursing the forthcoming dinner, I hopped out of my clothes and was heading for the shower when I decided that the 'gazooza' might make an interesting alternative. Bottles of perfumed bath essence were at hand and, vaguely remembering the manager's instructions, I climbed into the empty bath and annointed myself with one of these pungent preparations. It seemed the next move was to turn on a golden tap on the wall, which I did. There was a few seconds' delay, during which time I gazed about me in anticipation. I didn't have long to wait. Without warning, jets of icy cold water erupted from at least six points, some of which unfortunately were directly beneath me. The second most immediate effect was that the bath oil with which I was covered produced a swirling mass of bubbles. Unable to withstand one particular jet that was squirting directly upwards, I tried to escape from the bath, only to be struck in the face by another geyser. The water was now painfully hot and the steam level had increased to such a degree that I could no longer read any instructions which might enable me to turn the confounded thing off. By a Herculean effort I managed to slither over the edge of the bath but attempts at standing were thwarted by the bath oil, and I fell flat on my back. Whilst lying winded in this ridiculous posture, I perceived a charming black maid in her sixties peering at me through the steam.

'You gotta problem, sir?' she enquired, to which I replied: 'Turn the bloody thing off – please!'

By now the entire room was one gigantic bubble bath and I was slipping and sliding around the floor like a stranded sea lion. The maid calmly pressed a well concealed button and handed me a towel. I glanced at my watch and realised that within ten minutes I had to be making a major speech to an elite Houston audience. As I muttered some heartfelt thanks my heroine left, saying 'Yessir, those jacuzzi can be mighty dangerous – you'd never get me in one.'

James Bond films thrive on such scenes.

Before we sailed, our greatest task was to set up recruiting and selection systems that would produce the Venturers. Overseas the selection would be left to local committees, but in Britain it would come under the personal control of Roger Chapman. Throughout the world the same criteria applied: we wanted young people who were fit, compatible, could communicate in English and could swim five hundred yards. We were also looking for individuals with a spark of leadership and a willingness to place service before self.

We planned to select 1500 Venturers from Britain, 1500 from the USA and 1000 from the rest of the world. There was always the danger that this might become an expedition for the elite, and I suppose that if you are looking for young leaders that is an inevitable criticism. But our selection procedure in Britain was designed to lean in favour of the underprivileged who had had no previous opportunities to develop in any environment other than their inner city blocks of flats. We hoped that 20% of our 1500 would be made up of such disadvantaged young people. We also wanted to give a chance to the partially disabled: from my experience on Operation Drake I knew there were many handicapped people capable of the most astonishing feats, so they too would be included.

As we had had almost 60,000 applicants for 2 years of Drake, at a very rough guess we expected around 200,000 to apply for Raleigh over its 4 years. Again, previous experience indicated that 40% of these would be female. The Venturers were to be selected through a process which included screening application forms, an interview and, for the finalists, a selection weekend in a wilderness area when they would be put through their paces under adverse conditions.

Roger had divided Britain into twelve districts, each consisting of five or six counties with their own co-ordinators and other helpers. Each district had two selection centres and a panel of experienced judges. Thanks to the generosity of IBM, a giant computer had been installed in our London HQ to programme finance, logistics and Venturer selection, but it was this last task which was to occupy it for much of its early life.

During Drake we had raised all the money to sponsor the participants centrally, something which had only been achieved with the greatest difficulty. Afterwards, however, the young had suggested that if they could raise at least some of the funds themselves we might be able to include many more people, and already a number of companies, including Vickers and Taylor Woodrow, had indicated that they would send selected employees. Now there was an indication of good support from the service clubs such as Rotary and Round Table, and many youth organisations, especially the Scouts.

We were very conscious that there would be many applicants who might be disappointed, so we produced a booklet which listed other adventurous self-development schemes that were available. This stemmed from one of the lessons I had learned at Fort George, where I'd discovered that young people were surprisingly ignorant about the opportunities open to them. Undoubtedly there were a number of well-established organisations who saw Raleigh as a rival, but in this way I hoped to make them feel that we were in fact complementary and trying to direct youngsters to them.

We believed it was important to emphasise to the press that this was not a holiday or a 'jolly', but a very serious expedition with serious aims. The problem of national advertising in Britain was overcome by the screening of a special TV programme, in which Prince Charles interviewed three ex-Young Explorers from Operation Drake, asking them what they had gained from the venture and what they had put back into life since. The Prince displayed natural flair as an interviewer and quickly got the youngsters to overcome their shyness and speak with confidence. The programme, shown by TV South, put over some very convincing reasons for supporting Operation Raleigh, and His Royal Highness ended by urging young women especially to volunteer. Throughout Britain a notice was shown on TV screens advising candidates to apply to any branch of the Trustee Savings Bank.

It had not been easy for us to find a nationwide organisation to undertake the promotion and distribution of application forms, but the problem was solved through the kindness of the TSB, the only bank with branches in every corner of the United Kingdom. Their enthusiastic support and considerable help has been a major factor in the success of Operation Raleigh to date.

By Christmas 1983 applications were pouring in and most overseas committees had got their own campaigns under way. The selection weekends started the following spring, by which time Roger's Regional

HQ volunteers had been hard at work. The tests they had designed were meant to determine character, initiative and a certain standard of fitness. We ran a trial weekend at Sherbourne Castle in Dorset, once the home of Sir Walter Raleigh himself. Lord Redesdale, an enthusiastic member of our Council, had persuaded some young staff of the Chase Manhattan Bank in London, where he was a director, to act as guinea pigs. The rain fell in rods, it was freezing cold, the food was terrible and it was almost impossible to light a fire in the dripping woods: in short, it was an ideal selection weekend. The bankers, by the way, impressed us all by their performance, our judges got some valuable training, and a good time was had by all.

Incontrovertible proof of the good times stands out in every line of this candidate's memories of his selection weekend:

> 0900 on a cold, damp morning in April, and I was wondering what I was doing standing in the drizzle in a National Trust car park, grid reference 094 326. Last night my friends were wishing me good luck in The Dog and Fox, and right now bed seemed a far more sensible place to be than the start of an Operation Raleigh Selection Weekend. Maybe it was just a bad dream – a thought that crossed my mind several times over the next thirty-six hours!
>
> As the last of the forty candidates were being dropped off by car and walking up the hill from the station, I looked round and wondered why I had been chosen. Everybody seemed so much fitter and more suitable than me. I was very apprehensive and worried about what was to come but my fellow 'victims' seemed very friendly so I decided to just grit my teeth, smile (if you can do both at once) and try and enjoy myself.
>
> 0930 prompt. Just as I was starting to relax, chatting to my new-found friends, we were brought back to reality with a start. An Operation Raleigh minibus and Land Rover roared into the car park; thus we were introduced to the two SWATs, Operation Raleigh full-time staff called 'Selection Weekend Administration Team' – we found several far more suitable but unprintable names for them – and fifteen men and women who were our volunteer Judges and 'helpers'! They looked the

Opposite: A candidate abseils down an office block, participating in Operation Raleigh's first 'urban selection weekend' held in Liverpool to select youngsters from deprived inner-city areas of Britain.

Above, below and opposite: Rope and water tests on selection weekends at Culford School in Suffolk and Gilwell Park, Epping Forest.

Below: Young physically handicapped candidates participating in a selection weekend at a specially designed centre at Churchtown Farm, Cornwall.

Above: Teamwork on selection weekends is crucial as tired candidates carry their makeshift raft in Walesby Forest.

Below: This girl's face shows concentration and apprehension before she attempts to climb an obstacle during her selection weekend.

Opposite: The 'nightline' exercise where candidates display courage, determination and trust as they follow a rope, blindfolded, through some very uncomfortable situations, at Bewerley Park selection centre in West Yorkshire.

Above: A muddy test at the Hawley Hard selection weekend.

Below: Precarious river crossings for candidates at Bury St Edmunds, Suffolk, and Porthcawl, Mid Glamorgan.

Above left: A blindfolded candidate at Gilwell Park, Epping Forest, follows the 'nightline', negotiating a variety of obstacles en route.

Above right: Karen Travers tests her nerves during a selection weekend test as Horace, a relatively harmless tarantula, crawls across her hand. Having passed her weekend displaying this sort of courage Karen later participated in the Bahamas phase of Operation Raleigh.

Below: HRH The Prince of Wales talking to selected Venturers on 13 November 1984 at Hull, prior to SES *Sir Walter Raleigh* leaving her home port to begin her epic four-year round-the-world voyage.

most hard-faced, unsympathetic group I have ever seen; my worries were confirmed as soon as they shouted their instructions organising us for the weekend.

We lined up and handed in our medical and swimming certificates. Every participant must be physically fit and able to swim 500 metres. Operation Raleigh's definition of 'fit' and '500 metres' defy all normal ideas.

Then for my first real shock – our rucksacks were tipped out on the ground, plastic bags opened, pockets emptied and literally every nook and cranny thoroughly searched. Goodbye Mars bars, chocky bickies, Karimats, cigarettes, matches, watches. The SWAT's brief was 'anything that would make life bearable on an expedition'.

Leaving our piles of open gear on the ground in the rain, we were herded over for our 'welcome' speech by the Chief Judge in cool, concise language. We were told to expect the unexpected (he was a master of understatement!), not to do anything dangerous ('like turning up', I heard muttered from behind me), to use our imagination, keep our sense of humour and enjoy ourselves. These last two comments stuck in my mind as I glanced over my shoulder at our piles of wet kit on the ground.

We spent most of the day running from check-point to check-point constantly pushed by the Judges. Their job was to keep each of us working at our physical and mental limits, whilst at the same time monitoring all our reactions to everything. The Chief Judge was the only one who knew anything about us; to the rest we were merely numbers and they had thirty-six hours to find out if we were the type of people they could work with in close confines and difficult situations for several months.

At each check-point there was a task to do, an assault course, a high-level ropes course, scientific surveys, construction tasks, community work and several other challenges designed to test our ability to perform tasks under extreme pressure. We learned to make ropes from grass, tie knots, build a shelter, and use map and compass to get from point to point.

Opposite: Rupert Good, selection weekend Administrator, demonstrates how to handle a snake before asking candidates to weigh it.

Towards nightfall we found the now familiar SWATs and their minibus where we picked up tyres, barrels, poles and ropes and headed for a lake. 'Construct a raft to carry your kit (first priority), and all your team (second priority), to the island, retrieve your supper, and head to the base outward bound hut at $G + R + 694239$. Your food will be washed away by the tide in half-an-hour.'

We retrieved the food – one rabbit, two yams, two sweet potatoes, a quarter pound of sugar and three matches – with two minutes to spare; pushed the raft back to the bank (there was only enough rafting equipment to take our kit) and did not even have time to get cold as we were walking so fast.

On arrival at the Centre, we were split into new groups – I had just made friends with an unemployed lad from Newcastle; a lumberjack, an undertaker and an economics student. They had been a super team – a greater cross-section you couldn't have found! But now we were all with strange people again.

Supper was great once we had worked out who was doing what in our new team. No sooner had I taken my first bite of rabbit and sip of nettle tea than all the organisers were back. 'Five minutes, kit on back, fires out, let's go!' was shouted, and before I knew it I was running uphill to the Centre, tea down the front of my shirt and trying to chew a rabbit leg as I ran!

'Goodnight' said the Judges after the tests . . . 'build a "bivvy" by your fire . . . see you at 7 am.' One of the lads in our new group was sceptical about getting any sleep – he had done this type of thing before. We all slept with our clothes on.

Sure enough, about one-and-a-half hours later, we were very rudely awakened and sent off to deal with an 'accident' several miles away. Carrying our twenty-stone casualty over the 'mountains' that had been flat yesterday afternoon was almost the breaking point of a couple of our team but, as far as I was concerned, we had done the worst part.

We arrived back at dawn, the Judge (now dead after two-and-a-half hours of our medical treatment and rescue) gave us some mackerel and disappeared, rather disgruntled, we thought, to face his egg and bacon. We cleared our bivvy site and had probably the best breakfast of our lives – braised mackerel and nettle tea! We actually finished our food this time and were ready to go before the SWATs were back – much to their disappointment! But they quickly formed us into new teams again for the start of another activity.

We thought by this time that we had done it all, and with our good breakfast we had wound down a bit. Reality was restored incredibly quickly as we went over the most devastating assault course I had ever seen. Armed with only an egg-spoon, a fifty-gallon oil drum (named for some reason Cotton-tail) and two poles (eight feet long), we followed a blindfold trail, crossed ravines, climbed scramble nets and twelve-foot walls, negotiated rope bridges, fell into mud-filled pools, swam underwater, wired plugs, sewed on buttons, did mind-boggling logic problems – all against the clock. Our team came second.

The Raleigh weekends contained a crop of nasty surprises for the would-be Venturers, and, as before, we found that the girls were most impressive in their responses. In one area the candidates climbed down into a Second World War underground air-raid shelter. The descent, accompanied by an expert, was via a concrete-lined shaft set on a windy hillside overlooking Birmingham. The candidates had been given a flashlight and a measuring tape and told that at the bottom of the shaft they would find a wild animal which was quite harmless if they were calm and sensible: all they had to do was to measure its vital statistics. A young female biologist was the first to confront the angry four-hundred-pound gorilla that shambled out of the darkness emitting awful guttural grunts and smelling pretty vile. Having a great love of animals, she overcame her fear and edged closer to the monster. Then she noticed that it wore a muzzle, which, it was explained, was necessary to prevent it from biting anyone. With some difficulty she obtained the required measurements and returned to the surface.

However, the sight of this pathetic creature kept underground and being used for this purpose bore heavily on her conscience, and she wrote a strong letter of complaint to the press. Immediately the cry was taken up by animal rights groups and our phone lines at HQ were soon buzzing with angry enquirers. Susie Long-Innes, our press officer, did nothing to refute the reports for several days, by which time the story was assuming national proportions. Finally, when it appeared that the whole thing was getting totally out of hand, Susie let the truth be known: the poor mistreated animal in the air-raid shelter was in fact a Royal Marine officer in a gorilla skin borrowed from a theatre. Everyone had a good laugh but alas our deception had been uncovered, and we had to think of another method of testing courage. So we borrowed Dr Anthony Ashe's pet tarantula, Fifi. She proved to be one of the most effective deterrents for the faint-hearted and wriggled across many a sweaty palm throughout 1984.

CHAPTER THREE

The Race to the Start

As we entered 1984 I knew it was going to be a close-run thing if we were to set out that year.

By now we had moved our HQ from a Whitehall basement to St Katherine's Dock where, thanks to the great kindness of Lord Taylor, we occupied a Taylor Woodrow building. By now, too, we had, or almost had, two ships. Our search for a sailing ship had ended with the discovery of *Zebu*. She'd begun life as a galleass in a small, busy Swedish shipyard and spent the next thirty-five years carrying cargoes of timber, salt and grain across the Baltic. During the Second World War she smuggled arms for the resistance movement and refugees. In 1972 an attempt to convert her for charter work failed; in 1980 she competed in the Tall Ships Race but later that year she foundered in a severe storm in the Channel Isles. It was in an English south coast port that a young couple, Nick and Jane Broughton, had purchased her.

They stripped out everything inside, replaced twelve frames and part of the stern, and renewed the decking. They scraped together all the money they could but it was only through the efforts of unskilled volunteers under the supervision of a retired eighty-five-year-old shipwright that this feat was accomplished.

Hearing by chance of Operation Raleigh, Nick had contacted me and we found that *Zebu* was more or less what we wanted. So, after Mike Kichenside, now my marine advisor, had examined her, we offered them a charter on Operation Raleigh.

Zebu's final refit was carried out on Oulton Broad in Suffolk. Here students from the nearby International Boat Building Centre volunteered for spare-time work; some were eventually taken on full-time after the completion of their training course. The forward accommodation was soon finished and, whilst the crew's quarters were being built, another group of shipwrights demolished and rebuilt the main deckhouse. Skylights and companionways were added as work progressed and a new main-mast made of steel drill-casing was stepped. Wooden topmast, yards and bowsprit were made from trees felled locally and, by the summer, the rigging was well under way. Nevertheless, when General Sir Harry Tuzo, former Chairman of Marconi and a most helpful member of our Council, visited her, he had to express doubts that she would ever be ready by 11 October. But the dedication and enthusiasm of the workers was extremely infectious and soon their numbers had been swelled by volunteers from the Territorial Army and many other organisations. Lady Arran, another Council member and already known by the media for her speedboat records, became Fairy Godmother to *Zebu* and persuaded many manufacturers to donate vital items for the little ship.

Final stability tests were carried out in late August, and with the sails all bent on at the last minute, *Zebu* slipped her Suffolk moorings and sailed for London.

We had already decided that our flagship, when we found her, should be called *Sir Walter Raleigh*, and had taken the precaution of reserving the name. The Shipwright's Company had provided a naval architect, John Hind, to assist in our search. He looked high and low for a suitable vessel and it didn't take long for him to come up with a number of possibilities. The best was called *British Viking*, a 1900-ton stern trawler and former factory ship, built in Germany in 1965. Vickers had later converted her into a North Sea oil exploration vessel equipped with submersibles, but she still retained the distinctive features of a stern trawler: across her after-deck a massive A-frame, originally used to haul nets up a sloping stern ramp, had been converted for the lifting of mini-subs. She had a cavernous hold that could carry expedition supplies and the former submarine base in the hangar could be converted to house landing craft. Her 3000 BHP diesel engine, driving a single variable pitch propellor, would give her the required speed. Able to hold fuel for 18,000 nautical miles, she had a remarkable endurance and her accommodation would carry up to seventy-three crew, HQ staff, scientists and Venturers. And there would be plenty of space for scientific labs, an operations centre, computer rooms and all the complex radio equipment we would need.

British Viking was owned by J. Marr and Sons, a Hull-based company. Alan Marr, quite reasonably, wanted £400,000 for her. All we needed was someone to buy her for us. For nine months David King and I sought sponsors, but in the end it was Hull City Council and the Department of the Environment who donated her to us. We desperately wanted to get our hands on the vessel, but due to prolonged negotiations it was not until April 1984 that we finally took her over, with seven months in which to complete a major refit and sea trials if we were to leave on time and maintain our programme around the world. The alternative was to postpone the start of Operation Raleigh by a year.

Working with Marrs and their subsidiary, Globe Engineering, Mike Kichenside had most of the refit planned by April. Already many kind sponsors had offered equipment and some, knowing that the former fish deck amidships was to be converted into an exhibition area, were already preparing displays that would be seen throughout the world. Money was as tight as ever and we now needed a massive labour force. It was a wet Sunday when Cathy Davies, now Second Lieutenant Davies, of the WRAC (Volunteers) arrived at Hull with her workforce of eight.

Cathy had still been at school, when a teacher, knowing her love of challenge and the great outdoors, had passed her an application form for Operation Drake. Against stiff opposition she'd gained a place and won a sponsorship provided by Prince Charles. She loved it: jungle, mud, toil and working with young men and women of many lands. They felt like young lions and when her stint was over there was no turning back, so she went as a junior member of the staff on another expedition in the wilds of Papua New Guinea.

Even though she had survived Operation Drake and Fort George, Cathy was daunted by the monumental task that lay ahead. Her team had volunteered to help transform the unwelcoming 'Sir Wally Rustbucket' into a logistic support ship and floating scientific laboratory. There were youngsters from the Youth Training Scheme, selected volunteers, some TA soldiers and a few day-released inmates from the local prison to help. The first task was to clear the ship of rubbish, the second to chip and re-paint the decks: on a 300-foot vessel, this is an enormous job. However, the group enjoyed the camaraderie, and in the evenings tired themselves out even more playing basketball and swimming. Unfortunately, they were sometimes so covered in paint remover, chipped rust and wood shavings, not to mention mud, that they were not allowed in the local baths.

I was thankful that there were so many companies in Hull prepared to assist; and the refit committee, under the able and energetic guidance of its chairman, Councillor Jim Mulgrove, and our county co-ordinator, David Hopkins, did everything possible to boost morale and keep up local interest. The people of Hull had quickly taken the ship to their hearts.

Back at St Katherine's Dock, things were not going well. There was a vast list of items to be procured, preferably free of charge, at worst at a hefty discount, and it was only the arrival of Anton Bowring that gave me any confidence that we should overcome this enormous problem. Anton had been doing a similar job with the highly successful Trans-Globe Expedition and although he had taken a little time off to get married and start a family, expeditions were still very much in his blood. It was a great day for Operation Raleigh when he became our Director of Supplies, ably assisted by Jennifer Watts and several other volunteers skilled at squeezing blood from stones.

The Merseyside County Council generously offered to provide two water-jet-propelled landing craft that would be built by apprentices working under the Manpower Services Scheme at Cammell Lairds in Liverpool, and the Avon Rubber Company agreed to give us the very latest of their six yard Searider inshore rescue craft. Robert Glen of E. P. Barrus, a long-time supporter of ours, persuaded Mariner Outboards to become Operation Raleigh's exclusive suppliers. This was a great step forward, for most of our ferrying and inshore work and much of the diving would be conducted with the fast and seaworthy Avon boats, which these engines would now power.

Rover offered us the latest in their line of Land Rover safari wagons, and we also had the splendid Suzuki 'jeeps' that we had been using to help organise the selection weekends; to this kind gift Gerald Ronson added a couple of motor cycles. In addition, there were two British Armstrong scramble bikes and, of course, a Raleigh bicycle. Aboard the ship was a large diving centre with saturation chambers. These were of little value to us and were ripped out to make more space, but we still needed a recompression chamber and this was kindly provided by Ric Farrington Wharton of Wharton Williams Ltd. The marine biologists needed their wet lab, and because the land expeditions would bring back masses of fauna and flora there must be a dry lab too. Stephen Sutton also insisted on a microbiological lab, and there was a vital need for a darkroom and a workshop as well as a computer lab! Acorn Computers, Gallenkamp and Pattersons helped us considerably in filling all of these spaces. There were many hundreds of other sponsors without whose generosity the ship could never have left. One of the first to be appreciated was Justerini and Brooks, whose scotch helped to oil many a cog and keep me sane. Without the assistance of Unilever I could never have maintained our international communications, and without the support of British Airways and British Caledonian Airways my world-wide travel to raise funds and enthusiasm would have been prohibitively expensive.

Whilst we fought battles in Britain, our international committees faced their own difficulties. Because the United States committee had 40% of the Venturers allocated, theirs was a fight to which I paid particular attention. I quickly learned that you cannot raise money or enthuse people in America in quite the same way that you can in the Commonwealth countries. It is to the lasting credit of our friends in North Carolina, Hawaii and Texas that after a great many false starts they were the centres that remained on target. It was largely due to the determination and persistence of Ann Smith and Mark Bensen that we managed to hold Operation Raleigh USA together. The problems in New York had been more difficult and many friends, like Sir Gordon White, had tried hard to get it off the ground, as David Pincus had done in Florida. Georgia was holding up, as was Colorado, where my old friend Kelvin Kent displayed the same tenacity he had done in the Darien Gap in 1972. California was another bright star on the horizon in the persons of Maurice Taylor, an Englishman, and his wife Carol. President Reagan had kindly sent us an encouraging message and this all helped to build up our effort in America; but the real difficulty of publicising and co-ordinating the enterprise in some fifty States remains with us even now.

In January 1984 the Prime Minister, Margaret Thatcher, was our guest of honour at a luncheon organised by David King, and it was obvious from what the Prime Minister said that she was a keen supporter of our enterprise.

There were nine months to go and the pace was quickening. Every day obstacles would be put in our way but by some miracle help was at hand. We worked on against the clock, with most people in CHQ rarely stopping before 9 pm at night after a twelve-hour day.

On the operational front there were always problems to overcome. We were desperately short of qualified staff but, thanks to the help of the Prince of Wales, Mr Caspar Weinberger kindly agreed to assist by allowing members of the United States Armed Forces to take part; the Australian, New Zealand, Panamanian and Portuguese services followed suit. Selection weekends, presentations to sponsors, overseas visits, testing of equipment and the regular updating of the press all formed part of the routine.

Whilst I struggled with the operational programme and public relations, David King and his friends were striving to raise as much money as possible. Our budget was very simple. Four thousand young people should each bring in $5000; this should give us twenty million dollars to spend over the four years. We just had to make our expenditure fit into that, knowing that we would have a cash-flow problem in the first twelve months when our expenditure would be at its highest. Top of our list of priorities was to find an oil sponsor to cut the cost of running the flagship, and here we were greatly assisted by Denis Thatcher's own company, Burmah Castrol, who generously donated lubricating oil to the value of £110,000. Back in Hull, our refit team were also doing what they could to cut costs, but as the summer advanced we were constantly having to improvise and compromise to meet our priorities.

Before the expedition could leave we knew *Sir Walter Raleigh* would have to have full-scale sea trials, and had the idea of combining these with a promotional tour of British ports. By September, the majority of the work on her had, by some miracle, been completed, so the time had come to rename her and give her a thorough testing. At this point our Chairman, General Sir John Mogg, decided to hand over to a sailor, and Vice Admiral Sir Gerard Mansfield, formerly Deputy Supreme Allied Commander, Atlantic, who had once lived in Raleigh House, Norfolk, Virginia, took over in time for the flagship's commissioning.

4 September was a marvellous day. Her Royal Highness Princess Alexandra won the hearts of the people of Hull and the members of Operation Raleigh when she commissioned the ship in bright sunshine

from a dais on the sadly dilapidated dockside. Perhaps there was a ray of hope in the hearts of the unemployed who watched as, following a close look at the ship, the Princess gave the word and *Sir Walter Raleigh* pulled away to the strains of 'I am sailing'. Although we only discovered it at the last minute, our Royal guest had a special interest in the Operation, for her daughter Marina had applied as a Venturer, had got through all the tests on her own merit, and would join us later in Honduras.

Leaving Hull, the flagship visited London, Southampton, Bristol, Plymouth, Liverpool, Clovelly and Dover before returning to her home port. In five weeks twelve thousand people came aboard and the skeleton crew hosted thirty-three receptions.

'It was a really tough time,' recollected Chris Mahoney, the Third Officer. 'The ship was not then licensed to carry more than forty-six crew, so the Venturers had to do watches and rope parties as well as spend the whole day scraping, varnishing, fixing the masts and scrubbing down below. At night they were suddenly demanded to be presentable for the functions and so underwent incredible changes and were hardly recognisable.'

At the first-ever reception on board, in London, the ladies' loos over-flowed, creating a six-inch deep pool of sewage in the appropriately named wet lab. The guests, instead of being greeted by sweet-smelling hosts, caught only fleeting glances of them as they whizzed past carrying buckets toward the stern of the ship!

On leaving Plymouth, the ship headed into her first bad weather and as she approached the notorious waters off Land's End, rolled more than ever. As is customary, the safety edges were put up on the galley tables, but those who had never experienced rough seas clutched their crockery anyway. One such Venturer, Hugh Baines, toppled over in his chair and instinctively caught the two potatoes which flew off his plate, soon realising they were steaming hot! Nearby two people collided and one fell into the rubbish bin with his supper all over him. Many suffered from acute sea-sickness; and Venturer Steven Rose is probably best re-membered as the only person who still ate like a horse even though he was constantly ill. Most people starve when sick, but Steven would invariably turn up for meals, eat a course, run up on deck to feed the fish and promptly return to the galley for the next helping!

On 3 October the ship docked in Hull for the second stage of the refit. There was a frightening amount of work to be done in just five weeks and now, in addition to the hectic daytime schedule, each night a Venturer and a staff member were required to keep watch on the containers and gangplank, as the ship was full of precious expedition equipment. A pal from my time in the Oman campaign, Major Charlie Daniel, had now joined us as Field Executive Director, in effect my second-in-command. I knew him of old as the ideal man to plug a gap, so Charlie took personal control of the final stages of preparation; without his drive and initiative we could never have sailed.

The Venturers for Operation Raleigh's first phase arrived in early November, somewhat stunned that so much work was still needed but joining forces with the original work party for the monumental task of loading all stores into the hold. The night before sailing proved quite eventful: the Prince of Wales bar, kindly donated by Bass Export, received its final coat of paint at 0300 hours and, in view of the impending Royal visit, the ship was thoroughly searched by police who were then posted on the gangplank. Colonel Ted Carradus and Captain Jim Winter, two of our staff, arrived carrying heavy bags. When the police enquired as to the contents, they replied in unison 'Guns'. This was met with hearty laughter – but they really were carrying guns! Sporting arms and a few items for protection against the pirates we felt might be a hazard in 'certain areas'.

CHAPTER FOUR

America Next Stop

Much to my relief, *Zebu* was to sail a month ahead of the flagship's launch and the day of her departure for the USA, 11 October, dawned fine with a mild south-westerly blowing, just what we needed to get *Zebu* down the Thames and safely under Tower Bridge.

To send the brigantine on her way, we'd invited none other than the arch sea-goon and Council member of Operation Raleigh, Sir Harry Secombe. At eleven o'clock we all gathered at Tower Pier, beneath the forbidding battlements which Sir Walter had paced during his long imprisonment. The little ship, looking spick and span with oiled deck, varnished rails and bright green hull, was surrounded by wellwishers and the press. Sir Harry, in typically jocular manner, cracked jokes by the score as he met the crew. The first sixteen Venturers, resplendent in their British Airways T-shirts, already exuded confidence from their period of working aboard. The first helmsman was to be Neddy Seagoon himself: donning my white pith helmet, he strode purposefully to the wheel, posed momentarily with the girls, then gave the order 'Cast off, lads, America next stop.' Sadly they could not take Sir Harry with them around the world, so after sailing majestically beneath Tower Bridge, *Zebu* turned about and came alongside Katherine's Pier once more.

A buffet lunch for our guests followed, then, after the appropriate church service, *Zebu* pulled away to rousing cheers. It was a significant moment for all of us, the sailing of our first vessel and a great beginning for our venture.

Everyone aboard *Zebu* already knew each other pretty well – impossible to avoid it when there are twenty-four people living within a space of seventy-two feet. There were no doors on the cabins, the largest of which, accommodating four Venturers and all their kit, was only six and a half feet square. Near-transparent shower curtains across the two heads, or toilets, gave little privacy; indeed, should opposite heads be occupied simultaneously, the occupants' knees would almost touch.

Nick and Jane Broughton were aboard, but Peter Masters, an experienced and well qualified skipper, was in command. Steve Hawksley, First Mate, had explained all the various halyards, rigging and sails to the Venturers, a set of names and functions not easy for landsmen to learn. *Zebu* has twelve sails, each with four to fifteen lines, all with a separate name and a specific home on the pin-rails around the ship.

'It was essential,' wrote Venturer Adrian Turner in his diary, 'to learn the various names and pin-rail positions exactly, so that at night in the cold and wet everyone could act quickly and precisely on orders.' Another Venturer in the crew, Vanessa Hetherington, commented: 'At night the only light on deck was from the moon and stars and it was like working blindfold. We simply had to know where everything was.'

Having negotiated the Thames Barrier, *Zebu* swiftly reached the Dover Straits and sailed along the south coast of England to Southampton in good weather for a final inspection by the Department of Transport, who demanded last-minute modifications before she could head into the ocean. Alas, a weather change for the worse forced her to await a break in the line of depressions which had started to press relentlessly up the western approaches.

By sailing two hundred miles west into the Atlantic, Peter Masters hoped to miss the brunt of anything the Bay of Biscay might throw at them. They all felt a little apprehensive being out at sea, but the arrival of a school of dolphins, riding and leaping on the bow-wave at breakfast time on the first morning, gave the Venturers an idea of what lay ahead in warmer waters. It was just the tonic they needed to divert their attention from the fact that for the first time, they were out of sight of land, and the weather was worsening. At the start the sea was just choppy, but soon they began to roll in a heavy westerly swell with the wind rising to Force 8 and the spray hissing from the halyards.

Venturer Marion Thanisch wrote in her diary: 'This time we're really at sea – there's no land anywhere. How frustrating not being able to stand still! Everyone's on the deck feeling sick. The bilge-water is coming up into one of the starboard cabins, it swells up 3 or 4 inches and then subsides again through the deck of the opposite cabin as we roll! The pumps don't seem to be able to cope. What on earth am I doing here?' Later she recorded: 'Force 8 from sideways on. The waves are enormous and *Zebu* is rolling around tremendously. Trying to sleep between watches is a complete waste of time. There's nowhere dry – especially the bunks!'

Seasickness is an awful experience at any time, but being on galley-duty for the day and being ill at the same time was purgatory. Each Venturer took a turn at the task as part of a six-day rota. Whilst the job was quite acceptable in port, many despaired of trying to work amongst the sliding pots and pans. Bread-making, balancing trays of steaming hot tea up the companionway or simply pouring boiling water into a pot, were tricks to make any juggler despair.

The crew was split into three watches, each working round the clock, four hours on deck and eight off. This took a fair amount of getting used to, but strangely the most anti-social watch – being woken up at 0345 to be on watch at 0400 until 0800 – turned out to be everyone's favourite. Once on deck, it usually took a few minutes for eyes to adjust to the darkness, while the watch leaders briefly discussed any change of course or information on the weather. A helmsman and a bow lookout were appointed and the ship's bell was rung as the new watch took over. Adrian remembers: 'If we were in a busy shipping lane or the winds were shifting, the night watches flew by, with everyone kept warm and busy sailhandling; but in the open sea, especially in the waters where winds were constant, we were very cold and watches dragged by. Conversation and hot chocolate were vital to keep us awake. We knew that the safety of those below was in our hands. So we swapped jokes, told stories and solved the world's problems.'

They reached La Caruna in northern Spain on 4 November, just half an hour ahead of a south-westerly gale which would have pushed them back into the Bay of Biscay. Peter had warned everyone aboard that this first stage could take a fortnight, although he never dreamt that it actually would. However, after sheltering from the elements for thirty-six hours, *Zebu* headed south to Lisbon where, five days later, friends from the Portuguese Sailing Organisation, Aporvela, welcomed her in.

Thanks to the help of the Gulbenkian Foundation, Portugal had joined Operation Raleigh, and *Zebu*'s visit was our first formal contact with Britain's oldest ally. Young Portuguese came aboard as supernumeraries for a cruise to the south, where an unscheduled stop was made in the Algarve for some urgent engine repairs.

Back in Hull, Charlie and Cathy were driving their teams to work round the clock to have our flagship ready for the Royal launch on 13 November. Almost everything was being supplied free, or as cheaply as possible, and it's not easy to work like that in a hurry, when you need to put pressure on people who are giving so much; but the kindly companies of Humberside responded gallantly to the entreaties of tireless Jim Mulgrove.

At CHQ, there were a thousand other problems to be solved each day. We had to make provision for the departure of the Tactical Headquarters, Tac HQ for short, which was to be my field organisation. We had to rob CHQ of a number of its experienced members in order to man Tac HQ, so we appointed Commander Sandy McCarthy, a retired naval officer who had recently completed a stint in the world of commerce, as chief executive to hold the fort at home. Nobody envied him the job. There were other newcomers to CHQ, many of them volunteers, who would help to fill the gap as Tac HQ moved aboard the flagship.

I knew I would not be able to be aboard *Sir Walter Raleigh* but, in spite of what many said, my decision not to cross the Atlantic had nothing to do with a childhood horror of sea-sickness! I needed breathing space to cope with the affairs of Operation Raleigh after the flagship's departure, and planned to be in America for her arrival there. David King, a much more experienced sailor than I, volunteered to go aboard in my place.

For many weeks Nick Horne, an officer in the Royal Tank Regiment, had been calmly and quietly making arrangements for the ship's departure from Hull, co-ordinating all the companies and personalities involved. While Lieutenant David Burden of the Royal Signals was exulting over the Hull Telephone Company's gift of a Marisat satellite telephone and telex system, and Sergeant Peter Ellis of the Territorial Army stocked the hold with five hundred tons of mixed stores, mostly donated by kind sponsors, for Nick the fact that the Prince of Wales was to see the ship off and sail the first few miles with the Venturers made for a few added cares, as did the organisation of a TV interview the Prince was to give on board.

Nevertheless, by dawn on that great day, most things had been made ready. Only the day before, our two landing craft had arrived from Liverpool to join the microlight aircraft, a gift from Carlsberg, in the hold. Twenty Venturers from various nations were embarked, though Captain Mike Kichenside was still counting numbers to see how many he actually had aboard. It had been an all-out race against time, which we had only just won.

Hundreds of selected Venturers from all over Britain crowded into the North Sea ferry terminal at Hull to await our Patron's arrival; ambassadors of host countries, the Hull City Council and many sponsors waited there too. The streets were lined with people, military uniforms and smart Sunday suits mingling with sweatshirts. The Queen's Own Hussars Band played stirring music – and aboard ship Charlie and Cathy were still desperately putting on the finishing touches.

The Prince's winning smile instantly gave everyone a sense of relief as he walked into the Customs Hall packed with Venturers. Their enthusiasm was boiling over and it clearly affected the Prince, who simply could not resist talking on and on to them. They loved meeting him, and I was reminded of what one youngster had said to me some years before: 'You've only got to look at him to smile.' I could see now how true this was: he has a wonderful way of talking to people.

Having moved amongst the other, equally enthusiastic guests, Prince Charles went aboard to inspect the ship, carry out his TV interview and have lunch with the embarked Venturers. Then, standing on the wing of the bridge, he made a stirring speech to the crowds gathered on the wharf below. Mike Kichenside had readied the ship for movement the instant the Prince gave the command, but somehow she started to slide slowly down the slipway during his closing remarks; typically, he joked and carried on. Finally he gave the order to cast off. The band struck up and *Sir Walter Raleigh* really moved away. As soon as she decently could, Cathy dashed to the other side of the vessel to see how some vital last-minute welding was going on!

To the crowds' cheers, we moved out westwards into the Humber, accompanied by two fire-tugs shooting their jets of water into the waning autumn sunlight. The skipper took the wheel and headed out into the setting sun; a few miles down river the Prince left us to return ashore and the flagship sailed on to its first port of call, and my first home, Jersey.

Adrian Troy and his committee, with great help from the local branch of the Trustee Savings Bank, had laid on a splendid party to welcome us there. It was the first of our major overseas receptions and the exhibition deck really began to earn its keep, its displays laid out to perfection by Simon Leafe from the Junior Chamber of Commerce. I well remembered the visit of *Eye of the Wind* to Jersey at the start of Operation Drake, and how we had discovered our first technical problem there. It is quite extraordinary how everything that went wrong on Drake seems to have recurred on Raleigh, in spite of all our attempts to prevent it. Sure enough, there was a problem in the engine room which delayed our visit to Guernsey by several hours, but the delay had no effect on the reception Mike Duquemin and his team, also with the help of TSB, gave us when we eventually arrived.

To the south, *Zebu* was heading for Tenerife for refuelling and to take on fresh food and water before her Atlantic crossing. Leaving there on 4 December, she headed south by south-east to catch the trade winds, which gave the Venturers some wonderful sailing. There was spare time for relaxation, reading, learning celestial navigation or simply looking out for dolphins and whales. Heading due west for the island of Antigua, they paused for a mid-ocean swim. Adrian Turner wrote: 'We had shark lookouts posted high in the rigging. It's quite unnerving, swimming in 5000 metres of water.' The days of the Atlantic crossing drifted by leisurely, but in one twenty-four-hour period they made a hundred and seventy-four miles.

One Venturer who impressed everybody was Annalisa den Englese, a totally deaf girl from Norfolk who lipread all her instructions during even the worst weather and, by shining a torch at people's mouths, on the darkest nights. In the end she was one of the very few to gain a coveted Royal Yacht Association Day Skipper/Watchleader certificate.

The radio gave warning of the approaching Hurricane Lily, so Peter Masters, knowing that the winds inside a tropical storm can reach upwards of a hundred and twenty miles an hour, headed further south. Lily was coming their way and they set full sail to escape. Luckily the hurricane turned and blew itself out, but to the north the flagship was not enjoying a smooth passage.

Chris Sainsbury, our chief photographer, writing in his diary, recorded: '414 miles out from Falmouth and our roughest day yet, with the ship rolling and pitching violently. Life is most uncomfortable for the soldiers of the reconnaissance team who live right up in the bows. For those who have found their sea-legs it can be very amusing, particularly at meal times.

'The Venturers are still standing watches on the bridge, or at least those who can still stand, while others are found rolled up into unhappy little balls, wishing they were dead. The sea is a spectacular sight, with spume blowing off the wave-tops and the wind gusting to ten knots. The angle of pitch on the propellor has been reduced in an effort to make conditions a little more bearable, but our course is taking us almost straight into the seas, so the ship is alternately surfing down one roller then coming to an almost complete shuddering stop as the bow vanishes in a cloud of spray, with the waves breaking right over it and soaking those taking a breath of fresh air on the bridge wings.'

Later he added: 'The staff, crew and Venturers were nearly all sitting or lying in the bar this evening because no one could stand up. At about 2200 we were engaged in the popular sweepstake as to who would be next to dive out of the bar en route for the rail to lose a few pounds, when an enormous crash above our heads devastated this cosy domestic scene. A particularly violent roll had hurled a landing craft off its rails. Ben Cartwright, who had been working every day on the craft, was in the hangar deck in seconds, along with Charlie Nicklin, the bosun. The situation was serious: about eleven tons of craft with two Suzuki vehicles on its deck was being swung around like a toy. The chains which had held it in place had come loose and had to be tensioned before any serious damage was done. After several hours most of the movement had been controlled using blocks, and it was safe to reach the chains between the two craft without running the risk of being crushed to death. Later, when the weather abated, came the task of jacking the trolley back up onto its rails.

'I thought this eventful day had come to an end at last and was having a cup of coffee with Chris Mahoney, the Third Officer. Chris went off forward to the heads and suddenly rushed back into the mess and grabbed the fire extinguisher. He had been steadying himself when the ship rolled and had burnt his hand on the bulkhead: all the clothes in the drying room had caught fire after a waterproof fell on top of the heater. The plastic clothing was giving off acrid fumes and the heat was intense. Nearby cabins were evacuated and it took two extinguishers to get the blaze under control.'

Next day the disasters continued: 'Charlie Nicklin and Ted Seymour, one of the Hull seamen, were doubling up all the wires and chains on the landing craft after the emergency job done the previous night. Conditions in the hangar deck were uncomfortable, with the freezing wind howling around and water splashing across the deck. Matters were made worse by the fact that the massive hydraulically operated stern gates were not completely closed. Using a crowbar, Ted was holding them together while Charlie attempted to lash them securely. With the movement of the ship this was proving difficult, and suddenly an ear-piercing scream filled the hangar deck. Charlie had got his thumb caught between the gates and they slammed shut, completely squashing it. Jane Dunbar, the ship's Orcadian doctor, had the unpleasant task of stitching the stump together.'

The weather never abated and between the Azores and Bermuda the ship was tossed about in a horrendous storm, with forty-five-foot waves breaking constantly over bows and bridge. Cathy and Charlie Daniel, two of the few free from seasickness, went down into the bowels of the ship to help Chief Engineer Dennis Wood mend a fuel leak. Dennis, a highly professional man, was extremely worried about a hundred tons or so of water and oil that had leaked into an area round the steering flat and was now well above the water line, creating an unacceptable state of imbalance in an already unstable situation.

It was late in the evening and most people aboard were wedged into their bunks, trying to sleep. Dennis, unable to leave his engine-room, briefed Charlie and Cathy on the exact location of two pipes that could be removed with a hefty wrench to take the unwanted water and oil into the steering flat and thence down into the bilges, from where it could be pumped out. The only problem was that the two gallant volunteers not only had to work in the cramped confines of the flat but had to let the nauseous liquid in on themselves first of all.

Cathy, a lady noted for her explicit language, gave vent to several Anglo-Saxon oaths which made even Charlie blush, or so he says. They managed to wrench the pipes free and let the deluge of water and oil envelop them. The incredible roll of the vessel hampered the drainage but eventually it cleared, and our oily pair picked themselves up, re-mustered their sense of humour, shook hands and headed for the bar.

The foul weather in the North Atlantic caused such a delay that we decided to divert *Sir Walter Raleigh* to New York, which was a little closer than our originally planned arrival port of Beaufort, North Carolina.

This was a bitter disappointment for our staunch North Carolina committee but they took it well, realising how important it was that the ship arrived on the very day that a vitally important TV interview with the Prince of Wales would be shown, coast-to-coast. The interview, by Miss Barbara Walters, had been recorded earlier in Britain and was guaranteed an enormous public. It centred on the Prince's ideas about young people and Operation Raleigh, and as such it was crucial to the launching of our major recruiting drive in the US. ABC had scheduled it for 6 December, so early that morning John Groves, Barry Fredricks and I peered at the grey horizon towards a long stream of inbound vessels.

There at last was the *Sir Walter Raleigh*. After 3528 miles, the flagship passed under the shadow of the Statue of Liberty whilst tele-vision helicopters buzzed overhead. Off Manhattan there was the traditional fireship welcome. Operation Raleigh had arrived in America.

CHAPTER FIVE

South to the Sun

(*Bahamas Leader*: Major Alan Westcob, Duke of Wellington Regiment)
(*Turks and Caicos Leader*: Mr Barry Moss)

Billowing banks of fog swirled about the Coast Guard cutter; visibility was barely fifty yards.

'Dead slow ahead, steer 110 degrees,' barked the skipper.

'Half a mile and closing,' rang out the Third Officer's voice as he scanned the radar screen.

We helpless landlubbers pulled our anoraks close around us in the freezing fog and strained our eyes. There was nothing to see and, apart from the noise of our own engine, nothing to hear. But somewhere out there and very close was *Sir Walter Raleigh*, approaching North Carolina as the first colonists had done four hundred years before.

'These waters are bleak enough in broad daylight,' I murmured, 'perhaps not the place to be moving around with visibility this poor.'

'Ship on the port bow and another to starboard!' Mark Bensen, our executive director in the USA, had a worried look. 'I hope they've got us on their radar,' he commented, as we edged through the swirling grey mass. It was a real pea-souper.

Just our luck, I thought, storm and tempest, an engine breakdown in New York and finally we get one of the worst fogs to hit North Carolina in the whole year.

Then we heard it, the deep throbbing of a diesel very near. Rushing to the starboard rail, we peered towards the sound. The cutter was nearly stationary in the leaden sea when suddenly, almost on top of us, appeared the words *Sir Walter Raleigh*, standing out in dark blue letters against a white hull. She was only thirty yards away but barely moving, thank God, and rolling slowly like a great beast in the slow swell. Somehow I managed to clamber aboard.

For an hour, sirens continued to moan and then, heralded by a brightening sky, the sun broke through and rolled back the banks of mist. The flagship's propellor churned and we headed into Beaufort; running out our recently donated cannons at the approach, we fired a thirteen-gun salute. The reply from shore was much more dramatic, for Mark Bensen had persuaded the US Marine Corps to turn out a battery of field guns, and as soon as the noise of our somewhat puny weapons died away, their first salvo roared over the harbour, sending a great smoke ring high into the sky. The Marines' timing was perfect: the final shot was fired just above our bow as we swung into the dock to the accompaniment of bands, flags and cheering people.

'Welcome *Sir Walter*,' read a banner, 'you're only 400 years late.' There were speeches and a waiting bonanza of gifts, including four twenty-one-foot Carolina skiffs, and we reciprocated as far as we could with a reception on board.

Just as we had been about to leave New York a dangerous fault had been discovered in the engine which caused a four-day delay, and the patient North Carolinians had once again to re-arrange their plans and keep smiling. For us, the delay in New York and now in North Carolina meant that the ship was compelled to refuel and leave again after only a few hours. It was very sad but they had to press on to Miami, to meet the Venturers destined for the Bahamas, and Turks and Caicos Islands. Unfortunately, the Florida US Coast Guard couldn't be convinced that we were permitted to carry deck passengers, so after some long and costly negotiations, most of the Venturers had to cross to the Bahamas aboard the ferry *Scandinavian Sun*.

It was time now to put behind us the euphoria of Royal send-offs and triumphant landfalls and concentrate on the start of the first of Operation Raleigh's overseas projects. Eighteen projects had been planned by Captain David Allfrey's reconnaissance team of the Royal Scots Dragoon Guards a few months earlier; to involve diving, scientific research and community work on the islands of Grand Bahama, New Providence, South Andros, Greater Inagua and Cat Island.

Thanks to the delays to *Sir Walter Raleigh*, David's advance party on Grand Bahama had been faced with the challenge of setting up a camp without stores that were still aboard the flagship. Thanks to the enormous support given by Jack Hayward and his port director, John Hinchcliffe, some empty houses were made available to the expedition leader, Major Alan Westcob, at nearby Barbery Beach. David somehow managed to borrow nine mini-buses free of charge from the Ford Motor Company and between them, he and Alan organised a rudimentary base camp. The Venturers cheerfully accepted the chaos and soon the camp was enlarged with fifteen cardboard 'igloos' from the flagship's stores.

Meanwhile, to the south-east, *Zebu*'s sun-tanned crew had almost forgotten the outside world. Each day the Caribbean Islands drew tanta-lisingly closer and they dreamt of palm trees, beaches and rum punch. After covering two thousand seven hundred miles in twenty-one days, *Zebu* reached English Harbour, Antigua, on Christmas morning.

Thanks to dozens of kind folk and in particular the local Rotarians, Christmas on Grand Bahama proved memorable. All the Venturers were taken into homes, and the next day, at a beach barbecue, I asked some Arab youngsters how they'd enjoyed themselves. 'Oh, very good,' they said, and introduced me to their host. I was somewhat taken aback to discover that they had spent Christmas with one of the leading Jews on the island – but then Operation Raleigh achieves success in many strange ways.

The base camp at Barbery Beach was soon humming with activity as the Venturers attended orientation lectures, briefings and diving assessments in preparation for the forthcoming underwater scientific projects. The patience of diving instructors David Hughes and Kester Keighley ensured that a reasonable number of them were qualified to start work on these, but alas, someone at CHQ had mistakenly told all Venturers that if they learned basic diving at home they could dive in the Bahamas. Ned Middleton, the chief diver, shook his head in despair.

'How on earth did the raving idiot who promised that think we could do it?' he moaned, as groups of plainly disappointed Venturers gathered at his diving centre. Probably by knowing Ned was the answer, because he somehow found a way to give everyone a chance, and although it meant several projects going a bit short of equipment, the gear was shared around. Over the next two months each Bahamas Venturer would work at two different island locations and, where possible, carry out both land and an underwater project.

On 30 December *Sir Walter Raleigh* sailed out of Freeport with a party of twenty-nine Venturers and staff under Lieutenant Nick Wiles of the Royal Horse Artillery, bound for Cat Island. Also on board were the members of the separate Turks and Caicos expedition, led by ex-Operation Drake Young Explorer, Barry Moss. They would be supported by *Zebu*, already en route from Antigua.

It was a bright, breezy morning when we dropped anchor next day off the reef-strewn southern shore of Cat Island and began our first amphibious operation. Scanning the dun-brown island with binoculars, I could see miles of jagged coral seeming to stretch on without a break. Corporal Phil Swadling soon had the searider *St David* over the side and, carefully watching the echo-sounder, we headed through the turquoise sea towards the rocky coast. We made short work of the heavy swell and skipped in fine style from wave to wave, but it was a long search before I finally discovered the inlet where Nick Wiles, who had flown in ahead of us, was waiting.

Back at the flagship, Chris Mahoney already had the landing craft *Prince William* in the water and was gunning its powerful water jets towards the beach loaded with the Suzuki jeep, motor cycles, stores and more folded cardboard igloos. The seariders began to transport the first group of Venturers.

'Life jackets on. You'll all get soaked going in. But not to worry, we don't expect to capsize. If we do, though, stay with the boat, it won't sink.' Comforting words from the helmsman of *St George*.

Although the sun was bright, a heavy swell was running and each roller threatened to slam the landing craft up against the ship's hull. Most of the Tac HQ staff were also helmsmen, as were the ship's officers, so we took turns at driving the boats. It was really exhilarating, and everyone came back wet and smiling.

Though everything went surprisingly smoothly despite the swell, unloading proved a slow process. As the day wore on it became clear the job wouldn't be finished before dark, so a lithesome, bikini-clad Venturer was commissioned as a mobile, nubile lighthouse. Given a flashlight, she was sent to stand on the rocky headland to guide craft in. At 2130 hours the wind freshened. It was imperative that the flagship sailed at dawn to make the next rendezvous so the message went out to Nick Wiles on the radio: 'Sorry – you've had your lot – see you in a month.'

'OK, we'll manage,' he sent back, 'and, by the way – Happy New Year!'

Everyone had quite forgotten it was New Year's Eve – and had also quite forgotten about the mobile, nubile lighthouse, still flashing away from the headland. However, Charlie Daniel, gallant as ever, took *St George* in to collect the poor girl, who was frozen stiff and very hungry. As she waded out to the boat, a water snake slithered across her feet! Oh well, at least it was a little different from the London solicitors' office where she usually worked.

After that, the New Year was well and truly celebrated, many times over, as it occurred in all the home countries of those present. Amazingly the ship stayed on course, and I took the opportunity to telephone our World President, Walter Annenberg, in California via satellite and exchanged greetings with the guests at his party, who included the President of the United States!

At noon on 3 January 1986 the flagship edged cautiously towards the northern coast of Providenciales Island in the Turks and Caicos. There was a short swell and a strong breeze as the boats were lowered. Expedition leader Barry Moss had gone ahead and sent a pilot boat from Leeward Marina to meet us, otherwise the dog-leg through the dangerous reefs would have been hard to find. Landing the scientific Reefwatch group and the diving team who were to join *Zebu* took until well after dark. By that time Nick Horne had buoyed the passage with chemical light markers, but even so *St George* ran aground. Still, by 2100 hours everyone was safely ashore and the Venturers had made camp in some old buildings. Next day they would begin work on monitoring the deadly effects of the chlorine favoured in their work by local lobster fishermen.

Keith Jessop, who had gained fame and become a millionaire after his successful recovery of the gold from HMS *Edinburgh*, sunk off the coast of Russia in 1942, arrived to join the expedition. Keith, whose treasure hunting company had a contract with the local government, was to direct the search for wrecks along the south side of the Caicos Bank. With him on board, the flagship approached Grand Turk, capital of the islands, at first light the following day.

Fewer than ninety houses line Front Street, Grand Turk, none of them over two storeys high and most of them simple wooden frame buildings with corrugated roofs. There are the usual government offices, banks, shops, churches, public library and the lock-up, but of all the world's capitals, it must be the sleepiest and quietest. The Turks and Caicos are the least developed of the remaining British possessions in the West Indies: only six of the forty islands and cays that make up this dependency are inhabited, and its total population, mostly of African extraction, is only about eight thousand. There is little industry; the income is largely from fishing, off-shore investment and tourism. The Turks Islands, at the eastern side of the group, are surrounded by a shallow bank of coral and to the west, separated by Turks Passage, lie the Caicos Islands, cocooned within their own triangular-shaped bank some sixty miles long. The islands are virtually featureless with scrubby vegetation and little else: easy to understand why people say 'Where on earth are the Turks and Caicos?'

It is thought by some that Columbus landed here in 1492 and not in the Bahamas, but this is disputed. For many years underwater archaeologists have been seeking proof in the form of wrecks, most especially that of the *Pinta*, one of Columbus's ships believed to have gone down here. Operation Raleigh's own diving team were more than passingly interested in this and, based in a former American barracks still in reasonably good condition on Grand Turk, groups from the expedition were to be scattered throughout the islands. Nine local youngsters were to be included in the work, Operation Raleigh's first involvement with local Venturers. It was to be the first of many.

As the flagship drew close to the coast a cheer went up, for there, dead ahead, rocking gently in the swell, was *Zebu*, her young crew already up for their morning dip. Thanks to the kindness of the local people, everything ashore was ready and I was surprised to meet up with two old friends of mine, Sheila and Robin Laing, who voluntarily operated the 'harbour radio', appropriately using the call sign 'Flagstaff' and working from their bedroom! After two days of hard work Barry and his expedition were all ashore from *Sir Walter Raleigh* and a new crew assigned to *Zebu*. Taking aboard her tearful ex-crew, we sailed north to a fantastic welcome in Nassau, capital of the Bahamas.

Alan Westcob's major land projects there included the construction of the Lucayan National Park near Freeport, and the restoration of The

Retreat, an old colonial house at Nassau whose gardens contain the world's second largest palm collection. Both projects proved to be mammoth undertakings. Undaunted, the project leaders with their eager workers quickly realised that these challenges had to be met and conquered if Operation Raleigh was to gain early credibility, and they set to with a will. By the end of January both teams were in full swing.

Under the direction of Sapper Captain Huw Parker and CHQ staff member Duncan Walpole, five thousand yards of walkway through the Lucayan mangrove swamp were complete and the construction of the viewing platform, and spiral staircases into the underwater caves, was in progress. Thanks to the arrival of twenty-five young American offenders on the Vision Quest schooner, *Western Union*, extra hands were available to help with the clearing of the mangrove swamp and laying the footpaths. When I'd confronted Alan Westcob with the idea of mixing these delinquents with those of the world's youth selected for Operation Raleigh, he'd muttered 'You must be mad.' But he was the first to admit how wrong he was. Those youngsters made a great contribution to the Lucayan project, were thoroughly integrated with and accepted by the Venturers and *Western Union* gave our people an opportunity for some sail training.

On this expedition, the inclusion of two cerebral palsy victims, Rob Jones from Britain and Virginia Boyd from New Zealand, was very much in keeping with the Raleigh concept, and both proved wonderful examples of how the severely handicapped can cope, given the opportunity. Having sailed from Jamaica to Freeport on board Robin Knox-Johnston's catamaran *British Airways* in company with other Venturers, both now joined in the land tasks. Rob in particular gained a reputation as a demolition expert in New Providence. Armed with a large sledge-hammer, aided and abetted by Corporal Dickie McAfferty, he became responsible for knocking down the old walls of The Retreat.

The Retreat project, handled by sixteen Venturers and five staff under British hydrographer John Powell, turned out to be a major re-build rather than a simple renovation. Supplied with timber, shingles and tools by Kelly's Lumber Yard, they attacked the problem with great gusto, extremely fortunate in having Scottish Venturer Paul Foggarty in their group. A joiner by trade, he provided the necessary expertise to complete the task. A very weary but contented Paul summed up: 'I have never felt so good in my life. To see a seemingly impossible job completed on time has made my trip on this phase of Raleigh worthwhile.'

Later The Retreat became the headquarters of the Bahamas National Trust, and was opened by the Duke of Edinburgh in October 1985.

Like expeditions of the past, we aim to take along with us on each three-monthly phase a number of artists to record events and places and discoveries that specially interest them. Though all our artists and photographers, trained or enthusiastic amateurs, have other responsibilities on each project, they make the time to paint and sketch and snap in all sorts of circumstances and conditions. The idea for 'Project Art' came from diving expert, artist and underwater cine-cameraman Ley Kenyon, who saw what an opportunity Operation Raleigh could be for young artists, and is already making plans for a touring exhibition of the best work at the end of Raleigh's four years.

The main underwater project in the Bahamas was a coral reef survey led by ever-smiling marine biologist Mary Stafford-Smith. We also tested an amazing sub-igloo, a clear perspex underwater house, kindly loaned to us by our Canadian chairman and leading diving expert, Dr Joe MacInnes. Eight feet in diameter, this air-filled sphere enabled up to three divers to swap information on the sea-bed. We assembled 'Iggy' in fifty feet of water off Grand Bahama, the main problem being that it needed nine tons of ballast to hold it down. Mark Bensen solved that by rummaging around the island for some old car engines to cut up. They made our smart igloo look a bit unsightly, but they did the trick, and 'Iggy' proved a fascinating and useful addition to our equipment. It caused a few surprises, too. Early one morning two divers went down to prepare for the day's activities and found to their surprise that 'Iggy' was already occupied: staring out at them was a large barracuda. The American Venturer, by graphic demonstration, urged on his British colleague to grab the fish by its tail and pull it out – see, like that, easy. To his utter astonishment, he did – and got away with it!

In addition to these projects, many smaller but no less important tasks were undertaken and completed. Several were masterminded by the Venturers themselves, including a survey of an Underwater National Park off New Providence led by Ashley McKinnon from Tasmania. Ashley's expedition had been thwarted for twenty-four hours while he experienced life in a Nassau prison as a potential suspect in a drug smuggling ring! He was in fact an innocent passenger travelling from Freeport to Nassau in a light aircraft which was impounded by the Bahamas police on suspicion. Happily the case was dismissed and Ashley, in true laconic Australian style, commented: 'Nothing like experiencing all ways of living in the Bahamas. I met up with some real characters.'

In February a large group of fifty-four Venturers and staff, led by Lieutenant Richard Horner of the Gloucestershire Regiment, set up camp at Kemps Bay, South Andros. Rob Palmer, an expert cave diver, was going to give all the divers an opportunity of swimming down into the unknown.

Throughout the island there were many unexplored 'blue holes' and, as well as providing adventure and challenge, the scientific value of our explorations was proved: many exciting new and rare organisms were discovered. The fantastic sights a hundred feet down in the underwater caves were literally out of this world. Who would expect to see a perfect fifteen-foot stalactite so far under the Caribbean? This was a project that really tested the values of Operation Raleigh as we had hoped they would be: teamwork, trust in each other, real contributions to knowledge – and fun in the process. Jennifer Shaw, one of the most experienced diving Venturers from Canada, certainly encapsulated the views of this tight-knit group by commenting: 'This has been a fantastic experience. The work was hard, challenging and there was always a chance that something would happen to cause the adrenalin to flow. We have achieved such a lot in such a short time. It has been an experience of a lifetime, which I shall never forget.'

Greater Inagua, the southernmost island of the Bahamas, five hundred miles from the Barbery Beach basecamp, was the remote site chosen for Sergeant Piers Edmonds of the Coldstream Guards and his team of sixteen Venturers. Their task was to repair the four-hundred-yard turtle-retaining dam. Conditions were challenging and unpleasant: much of the island consisted of saltpans and mangrove swamps. Within seventy-two hours the back-breaking task – moving over a hundred tons of rock – was complete. Speed wasn't a necessary part of the undertaking, but Venturers wanted to make time for a survival exercise, which included building a raft of flotsam to reach a remote islet half a mile off-shore. In such shark-infested waters, this proved interesting. Indeed, Piers had good reason to thank Venturer Liz Baker for a timely warning.

As Liz said: 'It was quite sudden. We were happily snorkelling along when this large grey mass sped past me towards Piers. All I could do was scream "Shark"!' The vibrations and her shout scared the beast, and it only bumped into Piers as it veered away.

The weeks had flown by and all too soon it was time to congregate at Barbery Beach for the task of packing up, and steaming on *Sir Walter Raleigh* to the Turks and Caicos Islands to pick up Barry Moss and his team. On 21 February we came into Grand Turk, collected one group, and then moved on to Providenciales to embark the remainder. But a severe easterly swell had developed overnight and it proved too dangerous to anchor off the narrow cut in the reef, so we had to move westward to join *Zebu* sheltering in the lee of West Caicos Island. Luckily, next day the wind abated and we were able to get close to Providenciales and pick everyone up.

The diving team had achieved great success, finding no fewer than fourteen wrecks. Although they found no gold, they did discover one cargo of copper coins and numerous cannon, and also salvaged a complete fifteen-foot USAF target plane which bore the interesting legend: 'Finder Will Be Rewarded'! The scientific research had gone well, there had been some interesting caving, the old Militia building on Grand Turk had been renovated, and a basketball court for the locals had been constructed at Bottle Creek. A large supply of sports equipment, collected in Britain by Phil Wells, the project's quartermaster, had been presented to the local high school, and it was obvious that the expedition had made quite an impact on this little community. I was especially pleased things had gone so well as this was our first major Raleigh expedition to be led by an ex-Young Explorer from Operation Drake. There had been a great many difficulties for Barry to overcome, not least avoiding complications caused by the drug-trafficking in the islands. As we left, we heard that the Chief Minister and several colleagues had been arrested in Miami for drug-related offences!

The groups working at the Lucayan National Park and The Retreat continued right up to the last moment, applying the final touches to their endeavours before Jack Hayward opened the park to the public. In his speech he commented: 'Operation Raleigh has done much for these islands. You have left us examples of your excellent work which I am sure will inspire the youth of the Bahamas to contribute to similar projects in the future.'

As we steamed away, *Sir Walter Raleigh* to the States, *Zebu* to Roatan, we heard over the ship's radio the wonderful news that Dr Armand Hammer had donated three hundred and fifty tons of Occidental fuel oil and that it awaited us at Houston. Charlie Daniel was already there, working closely with Ian Green and his energetic Texan committee who had amassed an enormous amount of supplies for us. At Houston, too, we collected our first team of US naval officers, then headed for Central America.

Above: Operation Raleigh's brigantine *Zebu* in Bahamian waters after an exciting crossing of the Atlantic.

Below: Operation Raleigh's flagship SES *Sir Walter Raleigh*.

Left: Captain Mike Kichenside, Master, *Sir Walter Raleigh*.

Below: Diving equipment displayed in front of Venturers and crew at Freeport, Bahamas.

Right: Venturers aloft on *Zebu*.

Opposite above: In the Bahamas, the two landing craft on board the flagship were in constant use to offload stores to various expedition sites dotted around the islands.

Opposite below: Constructing causeways during a community project at Lucayan National Park.

Above: To construct the causeways and paths, logs and chainsaws had to be transported through swamps.

Right: Bats on Cat Island, Bahamas, were examined to determine the frequency of rabies.

Opposite above: The Avon Searider, *St George*, driven by ex-Royal Marine Charlie Daniel, is used in rough Bahamian waters to move people and stores from ship to shore.

Opposite below: Venturers assembling the Reed Paper Group's cardboard 'igloos' in which they would live for the duration of the expedition in the Bahamas.

Right: The generous Operation Raleigh supporter Sir Jack Hayward (left) and his partner, Edward St George, testing ropes at an orphan children's playground built by Venturers on Grand Bahama. Sir Jack kindly provided all the equipment for the playground.

Below: Venturers offload a Suzuki from the Merseyside landing craft *Prince Harry* at a project site on Cat Island, Bahamas.

CHAPTER SIX

Something Lost ...

(*Honduras, Black River Leader :* Captain Bob Weston, Royal Signals)

It was to be a race against time and weather on a coast notorious for its hidden reefs and shallow shoals. Our plan, as I explained it to the small group of expedition members and boat crew gathered on the bridge wing of *Sir Walter Raleigh*, was to unload as much kit as we could that evening, with the bulk of the stores to go ashore at first light.

Mike Kichenside had already warned me that things would not be easy. As far back as the 1700s, the Black River bar had garnered for itself a reputation as a graveyard. Listening to him, I began to wonder whether we might finally have waded in over our heads, trying to put ashore a fifty-one member expedition on this inhospitable stretch of Honduran coastline. And once landed, establishing even a temporary settlement might prove hard. In 1732 a handful of English colonists had tried to establish themselves here. A small British enclave on an otherwise Hispanic coast, the ill-fated Black River colony had been twice burned and finally abandoned. I stared across the line of breakers to where the shore lay, a thin swathe of jungle pressed beneath a sky of leaden grey.

We anchored around three that afternoon. It had taken the bridge some time to locate the narrow break in the bar that marked the lagoon entrance. Guiding ourselves in by the smoke of an unseen village, we then, after some searching, spotted the two bright orange panel markers set up by our advance party. While the rest of the crew stood by, I took in the Avon searider *St David* to gauge the strength of the surf and land a small beach team who would provide shore support and radio communication during the unloading. It was a rough trip, but the searider handled well, climbing high over the top of one wave to slam down into the trough of the next. We rode the surf for the last two hundred yards, a muddied green surge crested in dirty white. Through the spume of the

Opposite: On Operation Raleigh's first expedition in the Bahamas many scientific tasks were carried out. Here Venturers are constructing the Canadian sub-igloo. Divers can enter the air-filled chamber, remove masks, and confer under water without surfacing.

breakers I could make out brown sand to our starboard, and to port the unbroken green of mangrove. The lagoon entrance remained hidden until we were almost on top of it; we burst over the bar, scattering spray, and found ourselves suddenly in quiet waters. On either side the mangroves fell away to reveal clearings of palm and fruit trees, in the centre of each a thatch-roofed hut. I turned the bow in towards one of these clearings where Bob Weston and our liaison officers, Frank Dawson and local resident Herman Boch, stood waiting. The Avon nosed in beside a row of dugouts, beaching on a narrow strip of sand that fronted the clearing, and we stepped ashore onto the Mosquito Coast.

Though they had arrived only a few days before us, Frank, Bob and a wiry US Army sergeant had done much. The expedition's base camp was to be set up beside the grass-covered ramparts of the old Black River fort. Still strewn with half-buried cannon, Fort Wellington had been built back in 1748 to command the entrance to the lagoon and protect the infant British colony from Spanish attack. After the last Britons left in 1786, it was rechristened Fuerte de la Purisma Concepcion and rearmed to defend the newly formed Spanish settlement. Its guns, however, stood silently pointing out to sea at 2 am on the morning of 24 September, 1800, when hostile Mosquito Indians under their leader General Tempest swept out of the jungle, putting the town to the torch and massacring all but a handful of its inhabitants. It was this blood-soaked patch of ground that thirty Venturers from America, Britain, Hong Kong, Japan and Oman were to call home for the next three months.

Light was fading rapidly and there seemed little chance of our getting any stores ashore before dark. In Central America the gentle twilight of more northerly latitudes is replaced by a swift and violent sunset sliding quickly into starlit blackness. The advance party slept that night in the dirt-floored hut that was later to serve as their store. Describing the experience in his journal, one of them wrote: 'As we stood around the fire trying to get the rice water boiling in our mess tins, I noticed a crescent of shadows crouched just outside the circle of firelight. What must they think of us, I wondered, these strangers in their midst; visitors from another world. For myself, I felt comfortable in the firelit stillness. The log walls and palm thatch of the hut seemed somehow familiar, and it was good to fall asleep to the mingled roar of the howler monkeys and the surf.'

The next day was spent in unloading boxes of rations, erecting tents and generally transforming the clearing into a tiny outpost of our civilization. When I came ashore again later that afternoon I found the camp nearly completed: a village of tents and milling Venturers had displaced – temporarily – the pigs and chickens. Things progressed so well that by the time the flagship had raised anchor and set course for Panama, Bob Weston already had his first patrol setting off into the jungle. It was this patrol, led by Cathy Davies, which was to endure the hardships and make the dramatic discoveries described earlier.

For centuries rumours had circulated of a 'Lost White City' hidden deep within the mountainous jungles of Mosquita, one of the many El Dorados which had haunted the early Conquistadors and lured so many of them to their deaths. Cuidad Blanca had been the subject of search and speculation for the last four hundred years: local legends spoke of it lying somewhere in the sixteen thousand square miles of wilderness which lay over the mountains to the south-east of the expedition's camp. The patrol's archaeologist, Rowland Reeve, maintained a healthy degree of scepticism, doubting that a white-walled city of palaces and temples could still exist undiscovered even in so remote a region. Yet even he was eager to see what ruins, if any, lay on the far side of the mountains. So, on the morning of 19 April, the seven-member patrol set off upriver in search of 'the last great lost city of the Americas'.

They never found it. Instead, their searches revealed something in many ways more impressive. When they staggered back into base camp they brought with them reports of not one but a series of ruins, stretching from the coast to the uplands. This was to be our first indication that the Black River/Rio Paulaya region, long ignored as an archaeological back-water, had been the home of a sophisticated pre-Columbian culture similar in many respects to that of the neighbouring Maya.

While Cathy's patrol was foot-slogging in the jungle, those left back at base camp were far from idle. Scientific work on the coast had commenced almost immediately, with the senior archaeologist, Annie Robinson, and her survey team attempting to locate the ruins of Cape River and Mestizo Creek, two satellite settlements of the Black River colony. The natural sciences were also well represented and it was not long before the expedition's fish biologist, Peter Higgins, had his nets strung out across the lagoon. But it was herpetologist Mark O'Shea whose work attracted the greatest amount of attention, particularly from the neighbours.

The inhabitants of the quiet, lagoonside village of Palacios were not at all accustomed to the sight of *gringos*, much less *gringos* with wild red hair and great tangled beards. Add to this Mark's penchant for slithering under the raised floors of local houses in search of boa constrictors and you can begin to understand something of the impression he produced.

'They all thought I was crazy. For a start they don't see many big red beards in the jungle, and someone who would rather catch snakes alive than chop them up with a machete must have seemed very strange indeed.'

Before long Mark's snake-handling abilities and his apparent indifference to snake bites made him a local legend, an honour of which he was blithely unaware until the day the local witch doctor came to call.

'He asked me what my secret was. The native Hondurans, you see, consider every snake to be deadly. I tried to explain that not all snakes are venomous, but I don't think I convinced him.'

As work on the expedition's scientific projects progressed, the staff and Venturers moved their base farther upriver onto a sandbar twenty miles from the coast. From here teams of Venturers moved up small tributaries or along narrow jungle trails: no roads exist in the mountainous rainforests of the Mosquita, and all movement had to be undertaken on foot or in small boats.

The natives of the region travel its rivers in slender dugouts called *cayucos*. Early each morning a straggling procession of these, laden to the gunwales with stalks of green plantains, would slip quietly past the jungle camp on their way downstream. We wondered what the owners of these silent, slow-moving canoes thought of our Carolina skiffs and aluminium assault boats, all equipped with powerful Mariner outboards. Contact with the locals gradually increased as word spread of the small clinic the team set up at base camp to deal with minor ailments and injuries, and try to teach some elementary health care.

Among the many patrols sent out from the jungle camp was one organised by Peter Higgins to collect rare fish from pools high up on the Rio Guaraska, a tributary of the Paulaya. Peter, an ardent mountaineer as well as fish fanatic, combined the patrol's scientific mission with a more adventurous one by attempting an ascent of Mount Mirador, at

3696 feet the highest peak in the south-eastern chain. Torrential rains and impenetrable undergrowth blocked the attempt at the summit but not before Peter and his team of three Britons, one American and one Japanese had gathered a sizeable collection of fish, including two species which even the locals had never seen before. Mark O'Shea succeeded in capturing a six-foot long iguana which he carried about strapped to the top of his rucksack; at night it slept slung in a mesh net beside his hammock. On one of their last mornings in the forest, he awoke to discover that his pet had vanished, leaving the net perfectly intact.

Experiences previously unimaginable – a patrol stumbling into a green-lit jungle clearing to face a massive stone altar; a girl wakened in the middle of the night by a puma brushing against her hammock – became everyday occurrences to the Venturers. These experiences, however, were not without their price. The damp heat of the rainforest brought on jungle rot, tiny blisters that with time spread into open sores three to four inches across. Insects were a hazard too. On the coast the major problem proved to be jiggers, small flea-like animals which burrow into the skin of the foot to lay eggs. The only effective means of removing them was to make an incision next to the white, pea-sized egg sack and then squeeze. But in the interior the botflies were the real menace. They lay their eggs on the proboscis of mosquitoes so that they may be injected by the mosquito into a host. Once beneath the skin the tiny larva, whose head is built on the same lines as the bit of an oil drill, forces its way deeper and deeper and begins to swell until it is about the size of a maggot. The victims of botfly found that the only way to remove them was to smear the area with vaseline and cover it with adhesive tape. Starved of oxygen, the larva would begin to back out of the wound and could then be drawn painfully the rest of the way.

An experience one of the Venturers would rather forget had its beginnings when the expedition bivouacked just outside the small town of Las Champas. When they arrived the town was in the throes of a fiesta, the celebration of which seemed to involve much noise, a little dancing and a great deal of drinking. Some of our group joined in the spirit of the festivities and one lad, Tim Hulatt, a bit under the influence of the local sugar cane hooch, was prompted by a local guide to propose marriage to the fifteen-year-old fiesta queen. In the bright light of morn all but the headache was forgotten, and Tim continued merrily on his way upriver. It wasn't until many weeks later, back in Palacios, that the real after-effects of the evening finally caught up with him.

One evening, while a few of the expedition members were sitting quietly in a corner of the local bar, the doorway darkened and in walked three unusually large Hondurans, each with a shiny Colt revolver stuck into his belt. Seeing our lads, one of them strode over to ask if they knew a *gringo* named Tim who had proposed to their sister. It seems they wanted a word with him. To emphasise their sincerity they discharged their pistols into the ceiling!

Next morning when the rest of the Venturers awoke they found the camp in turmoil. A boatman had already run Tim out to an isolated sandbar, Cathy was hurriedly cleaning the 12-bore shotgun, and expedition second-in-command, Anthony Slessor, a fluent Spanish speaker, was sent to see if he could reason with the brothers. He returned some while later with the faintest hint of a smile disturbing his otherwise military demeanour. After much searching, Anthony had managed to track down the three Hondurans and discover the true purpose of their mission. It seemed they had been charged by their sister with finding Tim, to relate how much she had enjoyed his company, and how she hoped he would write to her after his return to England. The tensions in the camp instantly dissolved into hysterics, and it was a very sheepish young man who returned a half hour later from his refuge on the sandbar.

The expedition's final jungle quest was aimed at one of the archaeological sites discovered by Cathy's patrol. Annie and Rowland felt that this particular site, a large ceremonial complex, warranted further investigation, so everyone moved up the Rio Tulito for a fortnight to clear and map it. Mark and Peter were pleased, for the move gave them a good base from which to study the region's upland fauna.

The discoveries made at Tulito were indeed impressive. Stretching for more than six hundred yards along the river bank, the area of ruins contained twenty-two earth and stone mounds, an eight-by-thirty-yard enclosure formed of boulders up to ten feet long and weighing well over a ton; cobble-paved ramps; open courtyards; and massive, shaped stones, one with the face of a strange turtle-like animal carved in relief across it. The 'dig' was a fitting climax to the whole expedition. Once work was completed, the group tramped back to the sandbar camp and set off for the coast in skiffs, assault boats, Bellway canoes and rafts of bamboo, felled with machetes and lashed together with vines. One of these rafts covered the twenty miles back to base camp in twenty-eight hours, travelling on through the night despite the occasional appearance of inquisitive crocodiles. Most of the rafts, however, were not so fortunate. Many, caught by the swift current, were swept onto snags and broke against the huge drift logs, their passengers obliged to huddle miserably on the river bank, awaiting rescue.

Once back at base everyone set to, cleaning and sorting out the equipment in preparation for their eventual departure, and the scientists began to take stock of their finds, and write up the results of their work. Even they could not help but be impressed by the magnitude of the discoveries made in three months. By the close of the project, Annie, Rowland and their various teams of apprentice archaeologists had visited a total of fifty-six sites, and been told the location of an additional fourteen. Only nine of these ruins had been previously recorded in archaeological reports and fifteen were unknown even to the locals. The sites ranged from small riverside settlements to large ceremonial complexes similar to the one uncovered on the Rio Tulito.

Though no excavation was undertaken at any of these pre-Columbian sites, the survey parties did collect a number of surface artefacts which were given to the Instituto Hondureno de Anthropologia e Historia. Foremost among these was a collection of modelled pottery, including a larger than life-size mask decorated with elaborate tattoo-like designs. This object, similar to earthen masks brought out of the Mosquitia in the 1780s by an English traveller, was the first of its type to be recovered in modern times.

Mark O'Shea had succeeded in identifying over fifty distinct species of amphibians and reptiles. In all, thirty-five snakes were captured, including a pair of eight-foot 'Thunder and Lightning' snakes, caught by hand twenty feet up a mangrove. Mark's total collection represented over 25% of the known local species, a surprisingly high number, given that he was working in the dry season, when one is least likely to encounter reptiles and amphibians. Peter Higgins managed to sample twenty-four separate sites, and to collect and identify at least fifteen distinct fish species; the majority were sent back to the Natural History Museum in London for further classification and study. Sabina Knees, a botanist who joined the expedition late, nevertheless gathered an extensive collection of plant specimens both from the coast and the interior; her work represents the most comprehensive study of the region's flora undertaken to date.

Despite all the finds and all the challenges, though, by the end of the Black River phase the Venturers had all had their fill and felt ready to return to the world of hot baths and clean sheets. The Mosquito Coast, however, had one last adventure in store.

By the time *Sir Walter Raleigh* returned, the rainy season had begun. Sheets of steaming rain swept across the lagoon, and the seas beyond the bar had risen to white-capped fury. While most of the Venturers worked at dismantling tents and packing up, Bill Arnold and his boat crews began the dangerous task of running everything out through the surf. Bill, who serves as a lifeboatman at his home port of Troon, was no stranger to rough seas, and watching from my bucking searider as he weaved his skiff through the breakers, I realized that without the skill of people like him, the Black River expedition might easily have ended in calamity.

As if to bring the point home, one of the skiffs was swamped as I watched, and the sea washed its cargo away. Lieutenant Ross Nichols' rescue team worked like old-time Cornish wreckers, wading into the raging surf to drag ashore soggy cartons of rations. Through their efforts we succeeded in recovering all but seven of the eighty boxes swept overboard.

The roll of distant thunder blended with the crash of breakers as I ran the giant inflatable *David Gestetner* back to the flagship with the last group of Venturers. We'd battled our way out over the bar and I was just beginning to think we'd cracked it, when through the driving rain I caught sight of several people standing amid the waves!

'What on earth are they doing?' I muttered. Then someone shouted above the storm: 'They're on top of the skiff – she's turned over!'

The skiff, with Bill at the helm, had managed to struggle beyond the worst of the breakers but just as they seemed safe a rogue swell caught the bow, flipping it up and over. Luckily, most on board were thrown clear – everyone wore a lifejacket, naturally – and managed to clamber back up onto the waveswept hull; but Peta Lock, my personal assistant, was momentarily trapped beneath the skiff, her foot tangled in the cargo net.

'This is a bit too adventurous,' she spluttered as we pulled her into the inflatable.

Help, in the form of a searider driven by Third Mate John Pearn, was not long in coming. Fortunately, no one had been injured and the two boat crews, working together, soon managed to right the skiff and tow it to the ship.

Amazingly, we had managed to make it through probably the most hazardous of our expeditions to date without a single major injury. Bob Weston thoroughly deserved the large glass of J & B I poured him once we were all safely aboard. Still, though I was thankful this phase was at last over, I must confess I felt a touch of sadness as *Sir Walter Raleigh* turned her bow to the open sea, and I watched the jungle-clad coast fall away behind us and disappear in clouds of wind-driven spray.

CHAPTER SEVEN

The Sea and the Jungle

(*Honduras/Belize Overall Leader:* Major Anthony Stansfeld,
Army Air Corps)
(*Belize Leader:* Major Peter Marett, Royal Engineers)
(*Roatan Leader:* Captain Rupert Wieloch, 17/21 Lancers)

Operation Raleigh's Central American phase consisted of five expeditions. Our original plan had been to run only two in this region: one in Panama, to continue the work begun so promisingly by Operation Drake; and a second to penetrate the remote jungles of Honduras's Mosquito Coast. However, as relations between Honduras and its neighbour, Nicaragua, deteriorated, it became increasingly apparent that the planned one hundred-and-fifty-member expedition would be far too large to take into so volatile an area. Therefore, I decided to split the Honduras group down into smaller expeditions: one to proceed with the work originally planned at Black River, and a second to carry out diving and archaeological projects in the Bay Islands off Honduras's northern coast. The third expedition would be located so as to provide a firm base in the Caribbean to which the Black River and Bay Islands expeditions could withdraw if things took a turn for the worst. Belize, formerly British Honduras and a long-standing member of the Commonwealth, seemed eminently suited for this role.

Apart from its, to us, strategic position, Belize had much to offer. A country only the size of Wales, it possesses an immense variety of terrain from the savannas, swamps, lagoons and bushlands of the north to the rugged southern mountains carpeted in dense tropical forest, a jungle which in many areas remains totally unexplored, perhaps concealing undiscovered Mayan ruins.

Peter Marett, who had been with me on many epic ventures, set up his HQ in the YWCA building on the edge of Belize City. A small outpost on a coast lined with coral cays and mosquito-infested mangroves, Belize City has a distinctly colonial appearance. The newly arrived Venturers wandered its narrow, gravelled streets, past houses fronted by wide verandahs and along riverside docks where wooden-hulled fishing sloops mingled with our Avon inflatables and skiffs. After a night on the concrete floors of the Belize Defence Force drill hall and St Catherine Girls Academy, they set off for their project site in true Central American style, in buses provided by Batty's Bus Service. Each of these stalwart vehicles was packed with three tons of rations, assorted outboards, cookers, tools, water cans, wheelbarrows, life jackets, camp beds, mosquito nets and twenty eager Venturers and staff. Their destination boards bore some odd-sounding names: Bladen Branch, San Ignacio and Crooked Tree.

Crooked Tree, the most northerly of the task areas, lies about thirty miles north-west of Belize City on the shores of a wide lagoon. Its village was home to a population of only a couple of hundred souls living in ramshackle wooden houses set amongst mango trees and cattle pastures. The Venturers arrived here by bus and boat, the latter party having to haul itself the final mile across mudflats, and settled into the village Baptist Hall. Our leaders at Crooked Tree were an enthusiastic British lady police inspector, Vivien Mills, and Ian Jordan, a youthful and energetic schoolmaster. Their main task was to survey and cut a one-hundred-and-twenty-mile perimeter around a recently established wild-life reserve, and to construct a timber building to be the reserve's in-formation centre and store room. In addition, some Venturers were to assist in a lagoon fish survey by questioning local fishermen and examin-ing their catches. This project had to be abandoned when it was dis-covered that the fishermen had been landing their catch without paying tax, and were understandably somewhat reticent!

Once Vivien and Ian had been advised on the extent of the reserve, teams of Venturers went out on foot, horseback and in jeeps to cut a series of sight lines through the vegetation, and mark them with white-painted pickets or tree stumps. This sounds quite simple. In reality the young people soon discovered that the thick undergrowth was not easily penetrated. Each morning, cutting crews would trudge out into the brush and jungle, carrying with them all they needed for the day's work: food, water, cutting tools and paint. Some days the bush was so thick that only a couple of hundred yards could be cleared before the team, exhausted by the high temperature and oppressive humidity, would have to call it a day and return to base. There were indeed a few heat exhaustion and dehydration casualties to be evacuated, but in the end our weary but hardened crews succeeded in completing the entire perimeter.

Although construction of the information centre was not as physically demanding, it was no less difficult in other respects. From the start, the reserve authorities couldn't decide exactly how they wanted it built and the team arrived to find that no plans had been drawn up. Fortunately it was discovered that Venturer Judith Sayer from Wolverhampton was a trainee architect, so she was given the task of designing the building, and the Venturers set to work with hammer and saw to her specifications. Though obviously neither Vivien nor Ian possessed any knowledge of construction techniques, they trusted to the talent and skills of those few Venturers who did. James Hope, a carpenter from Sunderland, found his woodworking skills immediately in demand. He had arrived a quiet and unassuming young man, but when the others in his group saw that he knew infinitely more about the task than they, despite their academic qualifications, they pushed him to the fore and accepted his direction without question.

The Warden's Lodge was completed in two months, but with barely an hour to spare before its opening ceremony. The Venturers themselves had chosen its name and at the close of the festivities those attending, including the British High Commissioner, were invited to enter 'Raleigh Lodge'.

San Ignacio is a two-hour drive west of Belize City. Help the Aged International had asked us to build an old people's home there. As with the Crooked Tree project, construction experts were in short supply, but Lieutenant Robert Piper of the Royal Engineers and his three rotating teams of unskilled Venturers proved equal to the task, completing the foundations, pouring some of the concrete floors, putting on the roof and starting the verandah foundations. Fittings and work on the interior were left to the local community to complete.

The banks of the Bladen Branch River had been chosen as the location for the expedition's unique jungle camp. In the past this almost inaccessible region had been relatively ignored by scientific researchers, and little was known of what lay hidden within its thick jungle. Reaching the area after a four-day hike, the Venturers, under US Army Sergeant Patrick Traeger, established a base camp from which British and American scientists, assisted by the Venturers, could undertake their research. To help with jungle survival training, the Belize Defence Force had attached one of their soldiers to each of the three groups, and they proved invaluable in teaching the Venturers. Pat's work with the army had been in leadership training, and he put his experience to good use at Bladen: Venturers were nominated to fill command positions at the camp and to lead patrols into the wilderness. Young people who had never previously had the opportunity to organize anything soon discovered how difficult it can be to motivate a group of tired and hungry comrades.

Bladen Branch proved a fascinating place. Caves containing Mayan relics were discovered and an extensive Mayan settlement was located near the base camp. Work was going well. Then, just ten days before the third group was to withdraw from the camp, present-day cares recurred with a vengeance. Expedition headquarters received the radio signal: 'Heavy rains, river flooded, entire camp under foot of water.' A torrential rainstorm had caused the Bladen River to overflow its banks.

Peter Marett signalled: 'Abandon camp immediately' and began arranging an emergency airlift. Back at Bladen, the stranded Venturers had to cut a new helicopter landing zone to replace the one now underwater. Within thirty-six hours, during breaks in the rain, the camp was dismantled and its stores flown out. As the last helicopter lifted off, the sodden youngsters scrambled along the river bank and up onto the safety of the main road to begin the thirty-mile march back to civilization.

While they were struggling through dense scrub jungle in which, as one youngster described it, 'everything either bites, stings or grows thorns', our Bay Island Venturers off Honduras were slinging their hammocks between palm trees on a narrow crescent beach, backed by rainforest and facing the azure sea.

Their base camp on the island of Roatan, set up just down the coast from the old pirates' nest of Port Royal, was the staging point for diving projects among the islands' coral reefs, and treks across their rugged hills. Archaeological surveys and community construction projects gave each expedition member a taste of the village, the sea and the jungle.

Once *Sir Walter Raleigh* had unloaded the expedition, Leader Rupert Wieloch, a tough young cavalry officer, organised his thirty-two Venturers into eight-strong work parties and rotated them between the expedition's four major project sites. The diversity of backgrounds in the members of one such team struck me particularly: Stewart Crichton, a clam fisherman from the Orkneys; Dougie Taylor, an aircraft frame mechanic from Salford; Paul Hynam, a Pentecostal minister from Barbados; Heather Williams, a police officer's daughter from Weybridge; Wendy Binks, a potter from Perth; Simon Heading-ton, a hospital nurse from south London; Jeff Boath, a motorbike mechanic from Tyne and Wear: and Marina Ogilvy, 24th in line of succession to the throne of England.

Working beneath the crystalline waters of the Caribbean, the Port Royal groups dived on pirate wrecks and gathered data for our continuing Reefwatch programme. The climax of their time there was the three days spent aboard the forty-seven-foot St Pierre Dory, the *Ark*. Kindly lent to the project by American resident Randy French, this vessel allowed diving instructor Di Rosenthal to extend the Venturers' dive training to advanced levels which could not otherwise have been reached. Underwater conditions were superb, and by the end of the phase forty-five young people had managed to complete an average of twenty-one dives each, reaching an astounding total of nine hundred and fifty-four dives in all.

There was, however, one near-tragedy. This occurred during a carefully planned hundred-foot dive when one of the Venturers, Kathy Renwick, strayed away from her group and was next seen by another Venturer, Tony Griffin, lying face down on a coral outcrop at a hundred and thirty feet. He swam down and found her unconscious, but Tony was well trained and immediately carried out a controlled buoyancy rescue, bringing Kathy to the surface. Once there, help was summoned and she was quickly taken ashore; as her condition appeared serious, the MO decided to evacuate her. Luckily, a USAF plane was able to airlift her to Panama where Tac HQ arranged for a specialist medical examination and treatment in a recompression chamber. Thanks to Tony's quick thinking and timely rescue, Kathy recovered completely. His actions were acknowledged in November 1985 when he received a British Sub-Aqua Club Award.

The Bay Islands expedition also involved *Zebu*, recently arrived after completing her passage down from Jamaica. From April until her departure in mid-May she served as support vessel for archaeologists Mark Horton and Fiona Wilmot, and their teams of Venturers. Mark had served with me as archaeologist on Drake, and, although only twenty-three at the time, had been instrumental in many discoveries, including the 'Lost City of Acla' in Panama. Now, six years later and a Fellow of St Hugh's College, Oxford, Mark had agreed to take time out from his African studies to undertake a comprehensive survey of the archaeological remains on many of the Bay Islands. His discoveries are best described in his own words.

'During the ten weeks of our survey we managed to document a total of two hundred and forty-seven archaeological sites, over a hundred and seventy of which were completely new discoveries. Some of these were very large and extremely rich in finds. The sheer scale of pre-Columbian occupation on the Bay Islands far exceeded expectations. The evidence we collected suggests that before the arrival of the Spanish the islands served as trading posts – a vast market-place where goods from all over Meso-America were exchanged. A fascinating society developed to support this trading system, with numerous holy places, complex ritual sites, as well as hill villages and coastal fishing communities.'

On one sortie *Zebu* was, as usual, lying at anchor in a remote bay whilst the 'mad archaeologist' leapt about in the jungle, waving his arms with enthusiasm and revealing history at every step. Quite suddenly a squad of Honduran soldiers boarded the vessel, their officer demanding Peter Master's letter of permission to be in the area. Unfortunately, this was in Mark's pocket ashore. Peter could not speak Spanish to explain this, but could understand the officer's peremptory order to sail to the nearest port where the matter would be investigated.

'But I can't leave, all our people are on the island,' protested Peter.

At last the man seemed to understand and indicated that he would send his soldiers to round them up. The method they chose proved somewhat unusual: on sighting the Venturers, one of the men emptied his automatic rifle into the trees above their heads! They came in quietly but it was only by a stroke of luck that they didn't all go to prison, since the letter of permission didn't seem to carry much weight after all. A Honduran Government Minister happened to be visiting the Black River expedition on the mainland, and by good luck Mark was able to make contact and get him to speak to the soldiers by ship's radio.

Mark's teams also surveyed a number of colonial sites, including the ruins of Port Royal itself. This settlement had originally been founded by William Clairbourne, a companion of Raleigh's, who came here after establishing the Chesapeake settlement in Virginia. Raleigh, too, it seems, had an interest in the Bay Islands, and in the 1590s sent one of his captains, W. Parker, to the island of Roatan to explore the feasibility of setting up a colony there. I often wonder what Sir Walter would have thought of our own little colony, fulfilling his wishes only four centuries late.

Coxen's Hole, the Islands' major settlement, provided the setting for one of the expedition's two community construction projects. Here Venturers working under Lieutenant Larry Zoeller of the US Navy constructed a school for seventy bi-lingual local pupils – and Marina Ogilvy decided that the little town should be cleaned up, producing a vast quantity of dustbins that she made from old oil drums. Having painted them blue and white, Marina set them up in the streets. Strangely, no great improvement resulted. When I asked a local official why they were not putting their rubbish in them, he replied 'Well, Sir, you see, dey is Royal trashcans and we is ordinary people.'

At the nearby port of Oakridge, Stuart Crichton supervised the restoration of a lighthouse situated at the busy harbour entrance. The Light had been out of operation for seven years but in a week Stuart's team rebuilt and equipped it with a solar-powered light system kindly donated by Britain's AB Pharos Marine.

Another Oakridge project which proved immensely successful was undertaken by newly qualified doctor Chris Henry and Fiona Neve, a nurse from Hindhead, Surrey. They refurbished and ran a clinic for two and a half months, and gave the locals some training in basic health care. After making some repairs to the building and sorting through the clinic's drugs, some of which were unusable, being many years old, they opened up a day surgery and began making housecalls. One night the two of them negotiated a maze of channels in pitch darkness to reach a shack in the swamps where a woman had been lying in labour for thirty-six hours. A few minutes after they arrived she gave birth to a twelve-pound baby boy. During their time at Oakridge Chris and Fiona treated over three hundred patients and delivered two more babies.

It was typical of Chris that he should carry his Hypocratic oath far beyond the confines of his surgery, and remain faithful to it even when it meant endangering his own life. Woken late one night from his camp bed, he followed a clearly terrified Mosquito Indian through the jungle to a jungle hut where a badly beaten woman lay on the floor. As he treated her injuries Chris managed to draw from the man the story of what had happened.

It seemed that while he was away in town, two soldiers had broken into the man's house and raped and beaten his wife – he'd returned to find her lying on the floor. Even as the shocked man was speaking, the door burst open – the soldiers had returned to clean up loose ends. Brandishing their weapons, they informed the husband that they were 'taking him into custody', but before they could make a move Chris stepped in front of the man, shielding him.

'*Vamos, gringo*!' The soldiers' eyes glinted in the flickering lamplight. But Chris replied, in effect, you take him, you take me, and stood his ground. It was a warm, tropical night and the muzzle of the sub-machine gun felt very cold against his chest.

'This man,' said Chris, 'is not going anywhere until I speak to a government official.'

The soldiers refused either to leave or to bring an official and slowly the hours ticked by. At last one of them turned and disappeared into the night. It was almost dawn before he returned, bringing another man, obviously annoyed at having been woken at such an ungodly hour. One look at the woman, however, and he turned on the soldiers, ordering them to come with him. It was only after the three had left and it seemed certain that the Indian couple were safe, at least for now, that an exhausted and badly shaken expedition doctor made his way back to the clinic and to bed.

Not all of the expedition's work in the Bay Islands was as nerve-racking as Chris's adventure, but all of it, in some subtle way, served to change those who undertook it. As Venturer Simon Headington said: 'I'm afraid the hardest thing a lot of people are going to face is going home and discovering that even if they've changed, nothing else has.'

CHAPTER EIGHT

Fauna, Flora and Fer-de-Lance

(*Costa Rica Leader :* Keith Hamylton-Jones Esq, CMG)

'Squelch! Squelch!' Between two continents, between two oceans, after three days' torrential rain, the Venturers, up to mid-calf in mud, plodded up the thickly forested slopes of Barva Volcano. Recalling the first day's briefing, under a wide-spreading fiscus tree, they shook their heads in wonderment. Had not their weird expedition leader, Keith Hamylton-Jones, who wandered around talking Spanish and claiming, rather unconvincingly, to be the ex-British Ambassador to Costa Rica, Honduras and Nicaragua, told them that it was the dry season and urged precautions against starting forest fires? Worse: after Keith had further warned them about being mistaken for guerrillas if they strayed a mere twenty miles northward towards the Nicaraguan border, and about earthquakes, and how to deal with snakes, scorpions and sharks, had not chief scientist Dr John Proctor taken over the harangue? And had he not said that no living creature might be killed in the Costa Rican National Parks – not even the deadliest snake? Yet on the first day out had he not been among the first to reach for a machete when one of them was within an ace of sitting down on a bushmaster, known locally as a *Mata-buey* or ox-killer?

'These staff members are crazy,' they thought, and plodded on through the mud.

The Costa Rican expedition broke new ground. It formed the fifth part of our Central American phase but was our first expedition in a country where English was not the official language, and the only one in a land with no local armed forces to give logistical support. Furthermore, it was the first expedition whose main thrust would be scientific work in the rainforest, initiating standardized experiments to be repeated in Asia, Australasia and Africa. Many of our staff were from the British armed forces and I wondered how the services' encouragement of leadership and initiative would fit into the scientists' need for team-work on painstakingly repetitive tasks. The expedition would be a challenge, not only for the Venturers, but for us as well.

Due to a new 300% import tax, the four-wheel drive vehicles we needed for our resupply runs were as rare as dodos until the Ministry of Culture, Youth and Sports lent us an ancient Toyota and Michael Cannon, a friend of Keith's, provided a most useful Land Rover.

Seeing these loaded with stores and equipment heading northward up the pot-holed Route 9, the police became suspicious and, believing our people to be guerrillas, surrounded and raided the warehouse in which Chris Patterson (husband of our local chairman, Diane, an ex-New Zealand Young Explorer) had kindly loaned us as a store. A week later Captain Philip Richards, whom I had sent over from the Bahamas to help, was alone in the expedition's San Jose HQ when there came a knock on the door. Suspecting nothing, he opened it and found himself peering into the muzzle of a revolver. Within seconds he was gagged and bound to a chair whilst two bandits rifled everyone's belongings. Apparently Raleigh was on the hit lists of both the cops and the robbers!

To reach their first project site, the La Selva Forest base camp, Venturers helped Corporal Chris Jackson, Royal Engineers, to rig a ferry across the fast-flowing Rio Sarapiqui. Nancy Beavis of Suffolk recorded her first impressions of the primary forest: 'Tall, straight trees bursting into a myriad of greens . . . black sticky soil rich with the smell of decay . . . ferns and palms reaching upward, searching for splinters of light . . . at night a smothering cloak of blackness . . . insects' crescendo of percussion . . . pip and croaks of small frogs, a rustling and falling of leaves . . . moths as large as small birds flap helplessly around the light and mosquitoes whine a warning note.'

Having located some giant forest trees, they set about constructing two one hundred-and-twenty-foot high aerial walkways which would be used by expedition scientists to study species living in the canopy, 'where the great trees have their sex lives'. The presence of two nests of highly xenophobic black biting bees in the first of one walkway's terminus trees, a hundred-and-fifty-foot *Ceiba Pantandra*, was discovered the hard way by scientist Chris Bowden of Leeds University when he accidentally butted them with his head. When Dundee Venturer Neil Coupar followed him up the rope he wore 'my grandfather's old net curtains, dyed green and made into bags for face protection before leaving home'. From a platform in the forked crown, a line was shot over the second terminus tree seventy feet away. The second walkway, a hundred feet long and built to last ten years, spanned the gap between a 'diptorex' and a monkey pod tree. When our own scientists had completed their research, both walkways were left behind for use by the scientists and students at the La Selva Organisation for Tropical Studies. It seemed a small reward for all their support, and for the efforts of Dr Gary Hartshorn in securing the necessary permits for us to work there.

To the east, at Las Horquetas ('The Tree-forks') on the banks of the Puerto Viejo River, the expedition established Site 1B. Here the well-known Dr Tim Whitmore of the Oxford Forestry Institute superintended an exhaustive plant count and discovered no fewer than two hundred and thirty-six species on a ten-by-ten yard forest plot. Paul Walker, a wiry young biologist from Leeds, was netting amphibians after dark when he heard a cough and looking round he glimpsed a female jaguar and her cubs padding by! 'The silent are dangerous, the noisy safe' as Melissa Weeks of Australia was reminded, after fleeing before a snorting monster that came crashing towards her through the undergrowth. The monster proved to be a two-foot armour-plated armadillo!

On one of my visits to Costa Rica I met Paul Edgar of Hampshire, an expert snake handler whom I had last seen with a couple of pythons in a tent at TV South's Air Show the previous summer. Paul was in semi-paradise as he rushed off to show me a live fer-de-lance (*Bothrops asper*) that he had rescued when it was about to be decapitated by a local. He had been keeping the snake in his British Airways day-sack, which all UK Venturers had been issued with. Unluckily, Paul could not quite remember which one was his! Eventually, however, the right bag was discovered and I took a long-range glance at the creature coiled therein. The previous week Paul had witnessed a Costa Rican forestry worker, bitten by one of these killers, neutralise the effects of the venom by drinking an infusion made from the leaves of a local bush. The scientists were collecting samples of the plant in hopes of isolating its medicinal properties.

At another site a similar fer-de-lance, when not gazing libidinously at a coil of the expedition's electric cable, insisted on escorting senior research officers to the loo, which they found a trifle off-putting! The sex life of snakes became a point of study when Manuel Santana, a Salvadorean scientist attached to us, succeeded in taking the first-ever film of two bushmasters copulating. Fortunately Manuel was equipped with a video camera, for the process proved rather lengthy.

Chris Bowden used the walkways to set up ultra-violet light traps in *Pentaclethra* tree crowns to capture moths and flying beetles, with the object of analysing changes in their behaviour pattern throughout the lunar cycle. Richard Ranft, of the National Sound Archive in Britain, recorded the calls of no fewer than a hundred and fifty bird species, plus those of disc-winged bats and frogs. On play-back, Rosemary Burton, a Venturer from Houston, noted with interest that birds would fly out of the bush towards the tape recorder, thinking it was a potential mate.

'Even with three pairs of socks worn interchangeably . . . my feet have a very healthy culture of foot-rot and a colony of ticks has moved onto my body,' Rosemary confided to her diary. The concern of our apprentice environmentalists did not extend to conserving the life of ticks. Army insect repellent killed them but left them still attached by the mouth-parts, as did less orthodox remedies like hot needles and cigarettes. However, Dr Anthony Ashe made the useful discovery that toothpaste, liberally applied, caused the ticks to depart smartish!

During this time parties spearheaded by that of the indomitable Japanese Venturer, Hiromi Maehashi, pushed southwards to establish further camps, each at progressively higher altitudes, at which each team spent about three weeks. Their first camp, Site 1A, at 1650 feet above sea level, lay along the Sardinalito stream. 'The rain fell straight down, hard heavy drops that quickly drenched our clothes, plastering hair to one's face, mixing with sweat-trickles. Muddy boots slipped and scraped trying to get a hold . . .' recorded Nancy Beavis. At this site, Nalini Nadkarni of California University was studying ant communities and epiphytes in the forest canopy. Another zealous diarist, Catherine Murphy of Northants, described the scene: 'It was both exhilarating and frightening to perch on a branch eighty feet up and look across a sea of green tree tops . . . How insignificant our little camp seemed, with its two tents and tarpaulin-shelter!'

Camp 2 lay at 3300 feet, near the source of the Sardinalito but eight hours' hard walk from the base telephone, the team's only means of communication with the outside world. The quickest route was via a sun-baked deforested area used by small farmers and grazed by large white Brahmin cattle. It was a relief to be back amongst the trees climbing a ridge through cool dark primary forest, unusually spread with red and blue flowers.

The German Farmstead was the name given to Camp 2A, situated amidst towering forests at 5000 feet, this time near the headwaters of the San Rafael. The group had already recorded sightings of the forest's extraordinary wildlife – huge blue morpho butterflies, white-faced monkeys chattering, two rarely seen tayras, fox-like creatures, and the oropendola birds, 'their nests like coconuts in slings'. Now the volcano slope rose steeply and Camp 3, at almost 6000 feet, lay on more open scrubland between two more rivers. Here one might see male quetzals, their glittering green tails rippling three feet behind their iridescent bodies – for me the most fascinating birds in the Americas.

To the west of a cold lake in an extinct volcano crater, Camp 3A lay even higher at 8500 feet, just beneath the summit of Mount Barva. Around the lake stretched a dark, eerie world of mist trees where June Barcock of Kew Gardens explored and collected no fewer than two hundred and seventeen different species of pteridophytes, more commonly known as ferns.

After the rain stopped at Camp 1, the heat drove people out of the stifling tents into hammocks slung between nearby trees: at 3A there were frosts, necessitating extra blankets in the foresters' hut. Between the higher camps lay dauntingly sheer, forested river gorges; trails had to be cut laboriously by machete – it took eleven hours to get from Camp 3 to 3A. Re-supply involved Venturers staggering for a day under sacks of dehydrated food, cooking pots, aluminium ladders or whatever. Hairy tarantulas, surprised on the path, raised their front legs threateningly; red-and-black coral snakes, which chew rather than strike in order to kill, slithered away from the girls' feet.

At a camp near the Panama border, under coconut palm fronds beside the blue Caribbean, our project leader was cheery Phil Tong of Yorkshire, the first ex-Venturer to return as a member of staff. He was supervising work on the coral reef that, alas, was already 70% eroded by silt from deforested hills. Nevertheless 'swimming alongside the brightly coloured fish, lobsters and sea urchins was unforgettable. Like taking part in a Jacques Cousteau film!' wrote Neil Coupar in his diary. After days among yellow-striped angel fish, evenings were enlivened by the chatter of howler monkeys who threw sticks and droppings down on the Venturers. At night, the camp was prey to thieving coatimundis and raccoons, as well as fearsome mosquitoes. Edward Collins of Herefordshire remembers the moment that for him distilled the experience: as darkness lifted 'the dawn breaking over the horizon, its wonderful deep colour transforming everything around us. Between coast and reef a local fisherman is silhouetted, sculling his dugout to work. A sight I will never forget.'

'We have swapped rain and mud for intense heat and dust. It is four and a half months since it rained . . . the grass has long turned brown . . . there is an acrid burning smell in the air . . . towards midday skeleton-like cows stand languidly between motionless trees and insects take shelter from the sun's strength-sapping heat.' Thus wrote Catherine Murphy, camped on an inland plain, transferring her studies from zoology to archaeology. Archaeologists had discovered traces of a village chiefdom where maize-growing Indians had lived around AD 800 to 1500. Stripping off a small section of top soil, Catherine and the team uncovered circular cobblestone foundations of houses one hundred and ten feet in diameter. She remembered: 'a glistening layer of sweat mixed with the dust leaving grimy streaks all over our bodies . . . we look like Victorian chimney-sweeps.' Nearby lay grave sites in which, though the acid soil had eaten away the bones, it was still possible to estimate the height of the occupants (approximately five feet). A few surviving teeth grinned an unspoken message from the past. After work it was bliss to lie soaking in the Terraba River's rapids, keeping a weather eye on the crocodiles downstream.

To reach the only project site on the Pacific coast, expedition members faced a few local difficulties. They drove a hundred and sixty miles, then embarked on a boat journey down the crocodile-infested Sierpe River among mangrove swamps crawling with snakes, out past jagged rocks into the ocean and over a sandbar where thirty-three people had drowned in five years. Then they travelled across a bay to the north of the isolated Rio Claro near where Sir Francis Drake had landed in 1579 and where Operation Drake had planted a memorial four hundred years later.

The site itself, well beyond any road, was truly a paradise, but the project began with a crisis. The Drake Bay Development Association villagers had asked us to build them a bridge: their children could not get to school in the rainy season because the river was likely to rise twenty feet. Sketches received in London had specified a thirty-foot span. In reality the river was thirty yards wide, calling for a slight adjustment in the design! The challenge, as usual, proved a blessing in disguise. By lamplight Corporal Mike Bastow of the Royal Engineers, helped by visiting Canadian archaeologist Jiri Skopek and our own Chris Sainsbury, poured over stress equations. The result was a far better one-hundred-and-three 'pratt truss' box design.

In San Jose, another friend of Keith Hamylton-Jones, 'Chips' Filleul, the Canadian Ambassador, came to the rescue with funds from his Government for the extra materials now needed. On site the Venturers variously mixed by hand seven tonnes of concrete for the abutments or felled termite-resistant *amargo* (bitter) trees and shaped these into long beams, which they dragged to the bridge site with oxen. Work was ably directed by Lieutenant Jamie Hayward of the Scots Guards. When told that the bridge appeared slightly crooked, Jamie's instant rejoinder was that it only required a sergeant major to order 'Right dress', and all would be well! However, it was truly a most remarkable feat and a very fine bridge.

In south-eastern Costa Rica only seventy-five miles separate the Atlantic from the Pacific, and some Venturers undertook an adventurous march between the two oceans. Their route led them up the parched western flank of Mount Chirripo, from whose 12,000-foot summit one can look out across both oceans, and down the eastern gorges, across dense jungle to Phil Tong's diving camp. A heavily laden party, including ex-Paratrooper Mick Currie, expedition doctor Francis Arnstein and Sergeant Gaynor Avery of the Women's Royal Airforce Corp Volunteers, had been gone a week when newspaper headlines exclaimed 'Chirripo summit menaced by forest fires: three thousand hectares razed'. With no radio, the party was incommunicado and they remained so for seventeen anxious days. The fires had forced them off-course and they had been totally lost for three days, staggering up and down one-in-five gradients in the freezing damp and through rivers on half rations, because food provided by well-meaning Indians had left them bent double with giardiasis, caused by intestinal parasites. But they made it to the Atlantic. Shortly afterwards the Costa Rican Government declared Chirripo a prohibited area, withdrawing even their National Park staff.

In mid-April Nick Horne and I had left the steaming jungle of the Mosquito Coast and flown to see Keith in Costa Rica. At the same time the flagship came into Puerto Limon, where Columbus had arrived in 1502. There, thanks to the generosity of the Jamaican Consul, we managed to escape an astronomic berthing fee and that night held a reception on board for those who were assisting us in this delightful Latin American country. The Minister for Culture, Youth and Sports, Senor Hernan Gonzalez Gutierrez, flew back from Panama especially to be there, and his speech expressed the Government's whole-hearted approval of our work. His had been a personal as well as a professional commitment to Raleigh, for his son Adrian was one of the Costa Rican Venturers chosen by a tough selection process to participate and act as our interpreters.

Later Senor Gutierrez helicoptered onto a sandbank at the mouth of the Rio Claro to inaugurate Jamie Hayward's completed bridge, bringing Chips Filleul with him. It was gratifying to see how much the local community appreciated the work of the Venturers. Lesley Smith of Surrey wrote: 'Dark-eyed children manned the Canadian inflatable boat and villagers organised a football match and a religious service. At 1 pm, the hottest part of the day, we got very red-faced playing football whilst the local men ran circles around us. Women and children looked on in amazement that the girls could play too. Afterwards we drank *horchata*, a home-made almond and rice drink . . . for the service our 'heffy' (*jefe* = leader) was lent an English Bible and read a psalm; in turn the same psalm was read aloud in Spanish, we all sang and then Mario the priest thanked us, and God, for the bridge . . . and said that we would never be forgotten. He thanked each one of us in person, and really meant it. Villagers and Venturers hugged each other afterwards and we realised how we had helped the community and forged friendships – the whole purpose of Operation Raleigh.'

And so the teams closed on San Jose for the finale. By now Venturers were aware that in the *manana* culture-belt, enthusiastically promised buses or trucks might or might not turn up. They also came to realise that this, too, could be a blessing in disguise: the ordinary commercial bus service might not be designed for equipment-laden six-footers, but it did give them a chance to chat with friendly Costa Rican fellow-passengers.

On 9 May President Monge received the whole expedition, some hundred-and-twenty-strong, in the Cabinet Room for cups of Costa Rican coffee, photographs and words of sincere thanks. That evening Douglas Pilling of Philip Morris, and his wife Valentina, organised an uproarious farewell party by their swimming pool; they had been wonderfully supportive throughout. One of the Venturers, Andrew Castling, had hoarded one bottle of Newcastle Brown Ale for three months. Now was the great moment to open it, and he generously shared it with his friends.

After the expedition left, two Venturers remained behind in Costa Rica. John Shears from Devon and Angela Heaney of Durham would ensure that Operation Raleigh's work was not just a flash in the pan, but a lasting contribution to science. Angela was spending a year monitoring the rate at which trees lose their leaves, and John was on attachment to Costa Rica's Tropical Science Centre working on a NASA project, establishing ground truth for satellite imagery.

Tearful farewells to the rest of us from the locals showed that besides our community, construction and scientific work, we had also left behind sincere friendship.

CHAPTER NINE

Crossroads of the World

(*Panama Leader :* Captain Vivian Rowe, Royal Marines)

'Thees ees life!' exclaimed Captain Luis Puleio of the Panama Defence Force as he looked over the chaos which only the night before had been Operation Raleigh's base camp in Caledonia Bay. The departing Venturers nearby thought back three months to the first time they'd heard that phrase, back at the Jungle Training Camp in Colon where they had experienced their first taste of the rainforest. This short but comprehensive course, run by a mixed staff of American and Panamanian military personnel, had introduced them to the humidity, the mud and the insects that would be their all-too-constant companions for the duration of their stay in Panama. It had also introduced them to the swarthy captain's favourite saying, one which would accompany all their subsequent jungle projects and be heard most often when sunshine and high spirits were in short supply.

At Colon, at the northern end of the Panama Canal, the flagship had arrived to undergo some much needed maintenance arranged by our helpful agent John Bamber of Boyds Steamship, but first she would move the expedition to Caledonia Bay. Suitably acquainted with the jungle and its dangers, the eager teams boarded *Sir Walter Raleigh* and a PDF landing craft, and set out in a swell just sufficient to promote seasickness.

A sheltered natural harbour lying along the Caribbean coast of the Darien Isthmus, New Caledonia, had once been the site of a short-lived Scottish colony. Here, in 1698, the Scots had founded a settlement and built Fort St Andrew to defend it. The coming of the rainy season, however, brought with it disillusionment and death, for the region was rife with mosquito-borne malaria. Within the first six months a quarter of the colonists had died and before the year was out the survivors abandoned the site.

A second group, unaware of their predecessors' fate, arrived at Caledonia Bay only a month after its abandonment. They made a brave start but it was not long before a Spanish force besieged the settlement. Outflanked and outnumbered, the Scots were forced to surrender. A fourteen-day truce was declared, during which time the remaining colonists were allowed to board ships and set sail for home. Beset by storm and shipwreck, only a handful saw Scotland again. No further settlement was attempted on the Darien coast and the site was lost to the jungle.

In 1979 Operation Drake had located and mapped the remains of Fort St Andrew and divers working in the bay had discovered the wreck of the *Olive Branch*. A supply vessel bringing stores and re-enforcements to bolster the Scottish colony, she had burnt and sunk at her moorings when an over-enthusiastic brandy drinker accidentally ignited a barrel of his favourite spirit. Our present expedition had come to Caledonia Bay to carry on archaeological excavations at the sites of Fort St Andrew and New Edinburgh and to dive again on *Olive Branch*, with the aim of probing deeper into the life of the ill-fated Scottish colony.

Before the expedition's arrival, David Allfrey's recce section had cleared the old airstrip used by Operation Drake in the hope that we might be able to persuade the local airline to include it in their daily schedules. Despite initial high hopes and the continual promise from Panama City that the aircraft would arrive 'tomorrow', tomorrow never came. Instead, on many occasions, people and stores were delivered unannounced to an airstrip on a neighbouring island and had to be ferried across to base camp. The outgoing service was even more un-predictable: passengers had always to be prepared to leap into a boat and speed over to the island should an aircraft be seen making its approach. One group of visitors headed by the British Ambassador, Terry Steggle, spent most of their scheduled departure day marooned on the island waiting for a plane that never came. The following day an aircraft did land on the expedition airstrip, but the pilot refused to take the entire party. Thus, half were again deposited on the island to wait for the plane's return. It was only later that we discovered that a plane had indeed appeared on the first day, but earlier than expected. For want of the British Ambassador's party it had picked up a lone Cuna Indian and, to his surprise, taken him to Panama City. It is not known, however, whether he then made use of the Ambassador's car to go shopping.

Our excellent ties with the US forces proved invaluable when Michael Williams, a British Venturer ashore from *Zebu* on an island belonging to Columbia, suffered terrible head injuries after a fall. Initially the excellent first aid administered by two of his colleagues kept him alive until the Colombian emergency services could take over, but as we stood around the flagship radio I saw our senior medical officer, Jane Dunbar, was clearly most concerned. 'He hasn't much of a chance,' she confided as Bob Bradshaw, our US Navy radio officer, recorded the details of Michael's deteriorating condition. By good luck, our enthusiastic supporter, Terry Steggle, was aboard. It was just as well, for when we called for a USAF C-130 to lift a Briton from a Columbian island to Panama for emergency treatment in a US military hospital, we really needed this senior diplomat to cut through all the red tape. The Americans accepted the mission without hesitation and did a magnificent job. It was this timely rescue, and the skill of the Panamanian surgeon, that saved Michael's life.

When we landed the expedition at Caledonia Bay, the dry season was drawing to a close. The heat was intense and the ground rock hard. The picture postcard beauty was marred by one further discomfort – sandflies. These creatures travelled in near-invisible swarms of several thousand and possessed a voracious appetite for Operation Raleigh Venturers. Experts on their habits agreed that this winged menace seemed to prefer females, but appeared to be particularly fond of any variety of Japanese. As the beautiful Naoko Kishida put it: 'If sandfly in Japan, all Japanese emigrate.'

Caledonia Bay lies in the territory of the Cuna Indians, a strong and cautious people. Although used to foreign coastal traders, they are instinctively wary of strangers who stay amongst them, conscious as they are of the influence outsiders could have in threatening their independence and eroding their culture. It proved all-important for Vivian Rowe, the expedition's tough, softly spoken leader, to take great care in maintaining good relations with the local chiefs.

Once base camp had been set up, the Venturers started on their various projects. The largest of these was the diving work conducted on the wreck of *Olive Branch*. Captain Marc Moody, Malcolm Strickland and their underwater team trained and supervised the Venturers, ensuring that even the most inexperienced were able to dive in complete safety and confidence. Visibility in the bay was often reduced to zero in the silt-laden waters, and consequently much work had to be by touch. I had to admit that the black-bikinied WRAF corporal, June Liptrot, did bear a distinct resemblance to one of James Bond's ladies, and eyebrows were raised when she led visitors down into the murky depths saying 'Let me take your hand and I'll place it on something interesting.'

Work on *Olive Branch* was hampered by the failure of our suction pump, an instrument vital for the speedy removal of silt, but the divers continued excavating by hand, and entry was eventually gained into one of the holds. This resulted in the recovery of various of the ship's stores, including a number of salt-beef bones, a staple food aboard seventeenth-century vessels. Unfortunately the 'Cuna grapevine' converted these into human bones and a rift very nearly developed because of the expedition's supposed failure to inform the local dignitaries of so important a find. The Cuna chiefs took such an intense interest in the archaeological probjects that Viv was eventually forced to give them a full presentation on the history of the colony. Two Scots Venturers, dressed in kilts, went along to show the Indians what they'd been missing all these years. Fortunately for them, no bagpipes were available at the time.

As work progressed divers also located and raised three of the ship's cannon. Two of them, locked together in a massive coral concretion, were returned to the wreck for future archaeologists, but the third was taken aboard the flagship to Panama City to be displayed in the Patrimonio Historico Museum.

There seemed to be something of a jinx on the camp. When *Sir Walter Raleigh* had just arrived, I'd gone ashore to inspect the work on the airstrip and some old brick buildings which we'd asked our advance party to renovate for the base. The only people I could find were a couple of PDF soldiers who spoke no English. Then, to my horror, I saw the buildings – the blithering idiots, instead of cleaning them up, had knocked them flat! The soldiers looked suitably grave, waved their arms and cried 'Boom, boom!' Incensed by their wanton destruction, which now left the expedition virtually homeless, I took the men back to the ship for a full translation. Lisette Lecat listened calmly to their tale and said 'They're trying to tell you that there was a big earthquake yesterday and the buildings collapsed.'

So it was just as well they'd been unoccupied.

Later in the expedition our latter-day Caledonia Bay colony suffered from deteriorating weather: during one violently stormy night several of the camp's large marquees were flattened and a quiet dawn illuminated a shamble of sodden tents, kit and huddling bodies. Drastic measures were called for; an injection of 'Thees ees life', plus the knowledge that the rations were under one of the piles of debris, spurred people into activity. By mid-day a semblance of order had been restored and by dusk the tents were re-pitched in a manner which rendered them unlikely to succumb to anything less than a very determined cyclone.

One group of Venturers, unfortunate enough to miss the excitement of this natural disaster, had departed almost a week earlier on a jungle patrol. Their objective was Yavisa, a small town at the eastern end of the Pan-American Highway (at this point a rutted dirt track) which lay well inland beyond the rugged, jungle-covered Cordillera. Led by Nick Horne (ashore from Tac HQ for a leg-stretch) and guided by a PDF sergeant, they walked inland following rivers and streams up to the central divide. Their route had been carefully planned to follow water-courses for it was feared they might get low on water as many of the upper reaches of the streams were likely to be dry. Just to prove us wrong, heavy rain fell on the patrol's second day out and continued for the remainder of the journey.

High on the Cordillera, they moved into dense jungle. Progress slowed to a crawl and after travelling a total distance of only two miles in a day Nick feared that their rations would run out before they reached the re-supply point about four miles away. Fortunately, the patrol was able to make up time in a most exhilarating manner when introduced to the Panamanian military technique of floating downstream, feet first, wearing a waterproof rucksack as a buoyancy aid. They named this 'white water body hurtling' and used it, at one stage, to cover over

Above: The flagship transits the Panama Canal to begin the South American phase of the operation.

Below: John Blashford-Snell's field PA Peta Lock and accountant Neil Purvis (left) crossing a river in the Panama jungle on a patrol led by Tac HQ's Adjutant Captain Tony Walton (right) of the Territorial Army.

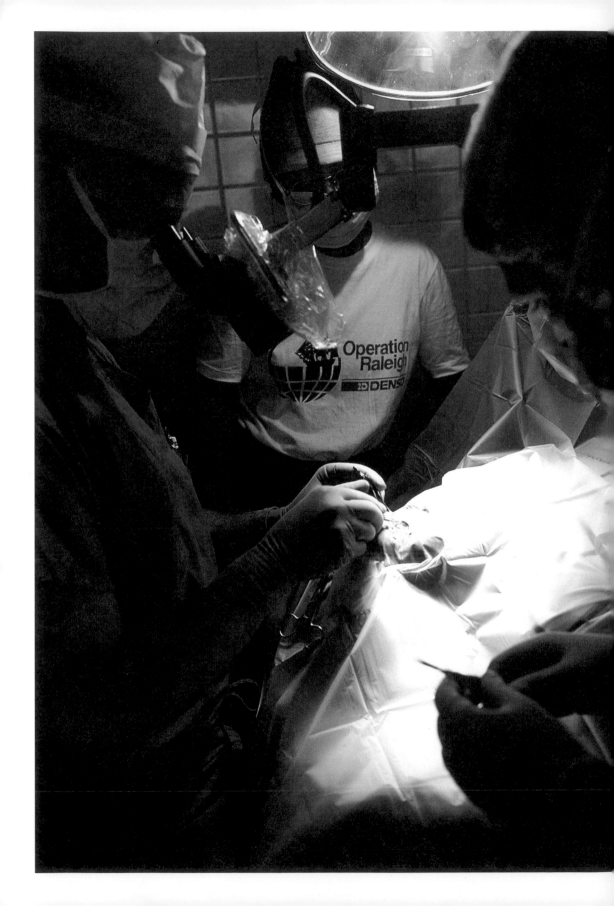

Opposite: Community projects in Panama included helping a group of ophthalmic surgeons from California to restore sight to cataract sufferers among the Choco Indians.

Above: A 30-metre bridge was designed (on the back of a cigarette packet!), built and completed by a small group of Venturers to unite two villages in the Osa Peninsula of Costa Rica.

Below: A young girl stands pensively on a river bank in southern Costa Rica.

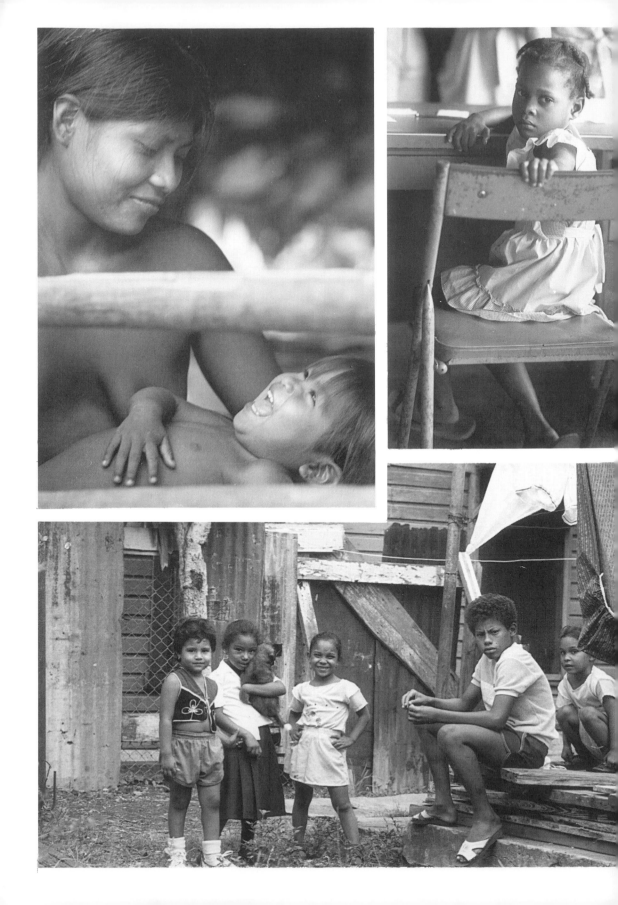

During their visits to Panama and Honduras, all expedition members became very friendly with local villagers, who were 'fascinated by gringos'!

Above: A Venturer ascends 120 feet to the aerial walkway to study the rich wildlife indigenous to the rainforest canopy.

Below: A bushmaster snake (*Lachesis muta*) being studied by scientists and Venturers in the rainforest of Costa Rica.

Above: In the rainforests of Costa Rica amazing varieties of wildlife were found, including this brightly crested royal Mexican flycatcher.

Below: In Costa Rica it was evident how useful were tests at selection weekends when Venturers actually found themselves confronted with swollen rivers.

Left: Chris Bowden, a member of the directing staff, checking instruments on an aerial walkway 120 feet above the forest floor.

Below: Lt. John Shears and a UK Venturer doing scientific research at La Selva, Sarapiqui River, Costa Rica.

eighteen miles. After a timely re-supply and a short rest in an Indian village, they hired a *paragua* (native canoe) in which to continue 'hurtling' and, after a continuous thirteen-hour trip downriver, stepped shakily ashore at Yavisa.

Their route along the Rio Chunchunaque had followed that of an earlier expedition which had ended in disaster. In 1858 a canal survey party from the US Navy, struggling through this jungle, had run out of food; their leader went insane, and the group turned to cannibalism to survive. This story was very much in the mind of one of Nick's patrol members, Lieutenant Commander Steve Butler, the senior US Naval officer on the flagship, who was almost certainly the first American sailor to go down this river since the tragedy.

At Yavisa they joined another group preparing for the visit of the SEE International medical team. SEE is a charitable organisation of opthalmologists under the energetic leadership of Dr Harry Brown, who travel to developing countries to perform cataract surgery and provide optical care for the indigenous population. Knowing that the SEE doctors would only have a limited time, the Venturers set to work to ensure that the maximum number of patients could be treated, transforming part of the small local hospital into a surgery and later helping Panamanian doctors conduct clinics at outlying villages.

With the arrival of the SEE team, Venturers made reception and treatment arrangements for the patients, helped in the operating theatre and conducted post-operative nursing care. Altogether over four hundred and fifty Indians and settlers were screened, a hundred and fifty nine of whom were prescribed spectacles and forty-eight of whom underwent operations for the removal of cataracts. In many cases, the blind were literally given back the gift of sight. Venturers and doctors watched in excitement as dressings were removed and patients slowly counted the fingers held up in front of their eyes. One near disappointment came when an old lady was found to be guessing at the numbers of fingers displayed. But, as an air of depression settled on the observers, a friend of hers explained that although she could now see, she had never learned to count! The SEE project was such a success that Harry suggested a similar one should be undertaken in Chile.

The Venturers now moved on to another project. Hands which had been employed so gently were turned to the slightly more robust task of rebuilding a school in a nearby village, swabs and tender loving care exchanged for hammers, saws and a degree of brute strength.

Back at Caledonia Bay, in addition to the diving, two simultaneous land-based archaeological projects were undertaken. Fittingly a Scottish archaeologist, Paul Flavell, undertook excavations on the ruins of Fort St Andrew. His researches revealed the sites of several of the Spanish siegeworks, including the main gun battery which had pounded the Scots into submission. Paul's archaeological partner, David Higgins, led the excavation work at the Spanish settlement of Acla, about seven miles west of Caledonia Bay. Acla is believed to have been the second European city founded on mainland America, very near to the starting point of Balboa's epic journey to discover the Pacific. Operation Drake had confirmed the city's location, but had had no time to excavate it.

David set up a small sub-camp at Acla in a belt of palm trees adjacent to the sea. The camp proved to be a happy experience for all concerned and relations with the Indians became much less formal than at Caledonia Bay. On one occasion David's group was invited to attend a nose-piercing ceremony. Transported in style by a large canoe, they arrived at dawn to find the whole village drunk. They never saw the child who was the excuse for the celebration, but that didn't stop them enjoying themselves. Sue Durbin, a petite Venturer, became slightly concerned when she was led away from the main party by a group of Indian women, but her fears were soon dispelled when she found herself being dressed in all the finery of a Cuna lady and then proudly displayed to her friends. After a long and exhausting day the group returned to their camp in a decidedly less stable canoe.

The most significant archaeological find made at Acla was the discovery of a small circle of wedge-shaped stones, the base of a round tower which had formed part of the city's defensive wall. The tower is believed to be the oldest European-built stone structure yet unearthed on the American mainland, and the discovery was given wide publicity.

The Acla site was not without other attractions. Giant leatherback turtles were discovered laying their eggs at night on the beach. Day-time archaeologists became night-time zoologists recording sizes of turtles and numbers of eggs, with biologist Val Snewin coordinating the data gathering. Some of the turtles proved bigger, nose to tail, than Peta Lock, my personal assistant, was head to toe.

Following the success of Nick Horne's initial jungle trek, the patrol programme continued with the aim of discovering old gold mines in Darien. Roger Haslop's team was given the arduous task of crossing the Cordillera at its highest point, Mount Anachucuna, before rendezvous-ing with a re-supply party at Churco Peje on the Rio Tucuesa. They were then to re-cross the mountains and proceed to the coastal town of Puerto Obaldia.

The first three days of the trek were almost idyllic, as they followed an easy coastal route and then turned inland. Their night-time camp sites were pleasant and relaxing; one even included a jungle swimming pool landscaped to a standard only nature can achieve. The going became more difficult near the summit of the mountains, and the constant cloud and drizzle made the nights penetratingly damp and cold. The vegetation thickened as their guide led them down the southern slopes following a steep, rocky river which had to be crossed many times. Progress was further reduced when a Japanese Venturer's leg became swollen and he developed an alarmingly high temperature. He staggered gamefully on, but after several days had to be carried into the rendezvous on a makeshift stretcher.

The re-supply party coming up the Tucuesa by canoe from Yavisa also experienced a mishap when their *paragua* was swamped in the fast-flowing river. Though all escaped without injury, a large portion of the patrol's rations were lost. Having recovered all that they could, the re-supply party carried on as high up the river as possible before beaching the canoe and sending a small group on a two-hour march to meet up with the patrol.

It was a hollow-eyed and haggard group which eventually reached the rendezvous. After the injured Venturer had been swiftly evacuated to the small re-supply canoe, the remainder took stock of their situation. They had insufficient food to continue on over the Cordillera so, after consultations by radio with Yavisa, they decided to abandon their crossing and make their way back to town along the banks of the Tucuesa. After a night in an Indian village they were able to hire a *paragua* large enough to take them downriver, but their disappointment at not having completed the intended route increased as they sat watching the mountains recede.

Several hours above Yavisa, at a ford where they expected to be picked up by a Suzuki jeep, they found instead their boss Viv Rowe, some new rations and a canoe pointing upstream towards the Cordillera. They were back in business and felt a great sense of achievement (expressed naturally enough with a chorus of 'Thees ees life!') as they crested the mountains at last and saw below them the panoramic view stretching away to Puerto Obaldia. After the rigours of their journey, however, so disreputable was their appearance as they entered the town that the local PDF commander promptly arrested them on suspicion of being Columbian drug smugglers. A quick explanation by the patrol's own PDF guides and a radio call to Panama City soon put matters right, and they were then made thoroughly welcome, and spent a pleasant couple of days resting and recuperating before our landing craft came down from Caledonia Bay to pick them up.

As yet no old gold mines had been discovered and so, back at base camp, this became the main object of the next expedition. Captain Howard Dyson of the Life Guards had been planning meticulously for the departure of this, the largest and most ambitious patrol, and his group set off from Obaldia, reversing Roger's route over the mountains to Yavisa. They were accompanied by the indefatigable Captain Puleio who, being the PDF's officer in charge of Indian Affairs, provided them with an excellent insight into the lifestyle of the local tribes. They were frequently entertained at Choco Indian villages and on one occasion were treated to the local version of mosquito repellent, an indelible blue dye which, though eminently suitable within the jungle, looked slightly out of place when the Venturers arrived back in Panama City – it took weeks to wear off!

Altogether, Howard's patrol spent twenty-five days in the field, covering over one hundred and twenty-five miles on foot and ninety miles by canoe before finally meeting PDF trucks near the Pan-American Highway. Throughout this period Kevin Mattison, the patrol signaller, had kept up daily communications with his partner Steve Carter back at Caledonia Bay. For a time the flagship's main radio was out of action and so Steve found himself coordinating all Operation Raleigh's Central American phase traffic from his tiny rattan shack. In his daily endeavours he was constantly watched by the beady eyes of a snake which had taken up residence in the roof, and spent each day wondering why Steve kept shouting at or trying to strangle all the reptilian radio handsets arranged along one wall. The snake had first revealed its presence by dropping onto Steve's head in a highly successful attempt to rescue one of the handsets which was receiving a particularly severe talking-to at the time.

Even before the return of Howard's patrol, the Caledonia Bay camp closed down and everyone boarded the flagship to return to Colon and thence to Panama City. They bade a fond farewell to their Cuna friends and to the slightly less cordial sandflies, both deeply saddened to see them go.

The success of our work in Panama had been made possible thanks to the help of many friends, not least the Kiwanis Club, who acted as our main support organisation, and especially thanks to the dashing and energetic Billy St Malo. Formerly Chairman of Operation Drake in Panama, Billy's enthusiasm was unquenchable and he worked with several of the ex-Young Explorers from Panama to recruit many youngsters and sponsors. We were also indebted to Robin Hardy and Tabacalera Istmana (the British American Tobacco representative) who provided our base office and happily put up with all their phones being jammed by our US army signaller's powerful radio! It was here that TA Major John Reed, who normally worked in the slightly more ordered environment of the British National Health Service, had struggled with all the complications of administration, and somehow kept smiling.

Finally *Zebu* and *Sir Walter Raleigh* sailed through the Canal. On our last day Billy turned up with a little donation – ten thousand cans of Panama beer which he felt would help us on our respective voyages in the Pacific. *Zebu* turned west to the Galapagos and Hawaii, and the flagship swung southward to Peru. Standing with our Panama Defence Force friends, Captain Luis Puleio waved us goodbye. 'Thees ees life!' he shouted.

CHAPTER TEN

In the Land of the Inca

(*Peru Leader* : Squadron Leader Mike Cole OBE, Royal Air Force)

It was the last time that Pam Gaffin, the tall globe-trotting American, would make the river trip to Puerto Maldonado. After three months in the Peruvian rainforest, her ten-strong team had piled the unstable *peki-peki* with rucksacks, rations and tents for the four-hour journey on the flooded Tambopata. As they climbed aboard, the muddy torrent hissed past, tossing huge logs like matchsticks in the spinning eddies. John, the boat's owner, pulled the toggle and the faithful Mariner outboard roared confidently. The frail craft swung out into the stream and soon they were absorbing the beauty of the emerald forest. No one spoke; all were sad to be leaving, even if it did mean going home.

Mother Nature gave them an unforgettable send-off, a magnificent sunset complete with sound effects from birds, insects and monkeys. The mighty river, now five hundred yards wide, pushed them on, its everchanging currents and whirlpools tugging at the hull. 'We sat enthralled,' recalls Pam, 'cameras clicking; but as the orange and red of the sky faded, darkness was suddenly upon us.' In fact, it was pitch black and they still had forty-five minutes to go.

Squatting in the now silent boat, the bow lookout swung a torch and strained eyes to differentiate between the shadows of swirling water and logs, or worse. 'Log! Go right!' 'Log! Go left!' came the warnings, and John swung the tiller. For a while all was well and a nervous calm descended on the crew. Suddenly came the scream 'Rock!' There was no time to react. With a splintering crash the *peki-peki* ran head-on into a great black slab that had appeared from nowhere. Water poured over the gunwales and people grabbed what they could as the craft went over.

'Everyone OK?' 'How far is the bank?' 'Stay with the boat!' 'Where's the boat?' 'Don't panic!' came the yells.

Pam thought: 'Oh my God, where are the cayman, the piranhas and the huge anacondas?' Her clothes weighed her down and it became impossible to make headway against the powerful stream. She heard John's voice crying 'I can't swim!' Nearly choked by the silt-laden water, she used her last ounce of strength to reach the dark shadow that was being swept along nearby, and there found six Venturers plus a half-drowned John clinging desperately to the *peki-peki*'s hull.

There was no sign of the other four, but soon they heard Kerry yelling that she was on the rock they'd hit and was staying there. Then came the faint cries of Martin and Margaret shouting from near the bank, and lastly they heard Jacqui, fighting with all the power she could muster to reach them. Her heavy hiking boots threatened to pull her down but she clung to her rucksack, which acted as a float. No one could help her – it was all that they could do to hold onto the boat that was trapped in a huge, slow-moving whirlpool, and stop it flipping again, when it would surely fill completely with water and sink.

Margaret's yells got weaker and weaker, then they stopped altogether. But now they heard that Martin was on the shore, looking for her. Jacqui was swept into the whirlpool and after a few circles she reached the survivors, totally exhausted, unable to speak. An attempt to swim the *peki-peki* to the nearest bank, three hundred yards away, proved futile, and now the cold was becoming a problem. They shivered and shook, knowing they must get out soon to avoid hypothermia. Then there came the unmistakable noise of a motor.

Sound travels far over water and it was a good four minutes before the boat appeared. They yelled and screamed like banshees – to no avail: clearly the boatman couldn't hear them above the noise of the engine. Suddenly Sara realised she had managed to hang on to the torch and amazingly it still worked. Now she flashed it at the oncoming craft but to their horror it veered away, giving them a wide berth. Then, just as they were beginning to give up hope, it turned and came slowly towards them. Its occupants were none too happy about picking strange people out of a river known to be well populated with drug smugglers, and it took an offer of twenty dollars and six gallons of petrol before they'd agree to rescue everyone. And even now the team's troubles were not over. The river currents were too tricky for the small boat to collect them all at once, so the group on the *peki-peki* was deposited on a small mud ledge sticking out from a cliff. Here they huddled, shivering and wondering if they'd ever be found again, as the ledge crumbled piece by piece into the racing water.

Kerry Kingston, the girl from Bedfordshire, was still on her rock, singing disco songs to keep her spirits up when the rescuers arrived, and eventually the Peruvians found Martin and Margaret too. No one was badly hurt, though Margaret had been rather battered when landing on the stony bank – but they were all pretty shocked. After more nego-tiations, their rescuers agreed to search for John's *peki-peki* and their gear, and surprisingly found a fair amount of it, plus the boat. Two and a half hours after the accident, the Venturers were on their way again, still shivering but singing as the tropical moon rose over Puerto Maldo-nado. Whilst they unloaded what kit they had left and thanked their rescuers, Liz ran up to the town to get transport. Afterwards Pam wrote: 'Standing ankle-deep in the mud, we looked up and saw the cavalry coming. Winding down the hill, headlights blazing, horns beeping, came ten moped taxis.'

As they entered the little hotel lobby, dripping wet, cold and exhaust-ed, Venturers who'd arrived earlier saw them and without a word dashed into action. Hot kebabs were thrust into their hands and as they were herded through the courtyard to their rooms for baths, a blizzard of clothing hit them as their friends on the balcony tossed down dry t-shirts, pants, socks and shoes. 'This is what Operation Raleigh is all about,' thought Pam. 'People coping with adversity and the value of friendship.'

On 13 July 1985, some sixty Venturers from seven countries had descended on Lima airport to start the first of our two three-month expeditions to Peru. At least that was the idea, but on the day only twelve turned up on time. The rest were scattered around Europe and South America in airline chaos and it was not until three days later that the whole expedition met together for the first time. This was but a taste of things to come. Their leader, Mike Cole, said that 'In Peru you either go mad, go Peruvian, or go home,' such are the bureaucratic and logistical difficulties.

He was absolutely right. Peru lived up to its reputation from the start when it became apparent that the stores off-loaded from *Sir Walter*

Raleigh were not only stuck in Customs, who had gone on strike, but were likely to stay there for a very long time, or at least until a little 'encouragement' had been given to release them.

Despite the efforts of the then President, Fernando Belaunde-Tery, who had come aboard the flagship for a reception and then invited everyone to his palace, the kit remained impounded. And so it stayed for the whole of the first expedition and half of the second, a total of some fifteen weeks. This presented enormous difficulties for the project leaders, who now had to face the prospect of going into three remote areas of Peru with groups of fifteen to twenty Venturers with only light-weight expedition kit and very little other logistic support. However, convinced of the basic good will of the Peruvian people and of the need of the small communities we were there to help, Mike was determined that the expeditions should go ahead as planned.

Back at Tac HQ in Chile, we were powerless to help: with the Peruvian banks, Customs and post office all on strike, it was impossible to get food out of bond, or money sent in to buy locally. The Venturers faced the problem heroically, pooled their money and managed to exist on only fifty cents a day each for three months. All suggestions of paying the usual bribe to release the rations were resisted, but when, on a direct order from the new President, Alan Garcia, the food was handed over to the expedition, the teams upcountry passed a message saying 'Don't send it; we're enjoying the challenge.'

Mike and his deputy, Squadron Leader Chris Bunney, had experienced the problems of Peru in 1982 when they organised a medical service to remote jungle villages, using hovercraft to travel up otherwise un-navigable rivers. Now they aimed to recreate this project in a different area at Puerto Bermudez. In addition, two other projects were proposed: building a bridge in a faraway northern province and undertaking conservation work in the tropical rainforest of the Tambopata Reserve in the south-east.

Travel to the sites was an adventure in itself. The expedition HQ in Lima became mildly alarmed after being advised that one group who had set out in a truck from Cuzco, the former Inca capital, bound for Tambopata – a journey that should have taken two days at most – had still not arrived eight days later. Just as a search was being planned, word came of their arrival. Apparently, despite it still being the dry season, the unmade road was axle-deep in mud for much of the way and they'd had to clear eight landslides and rebuild two bridges in order to get through.

The Puerto Bermudez team also set out by truck and took four days to reach there, driving through some of the most spectacular scenery on earth – first the totally barren desert that follows Peru's coastline, then a steep climb over the highest parts of the Andes before dropping down into the tropical rainforest region. Changes in climate and altitude took a heavy toll on a few members of the party and even the sight of their first llamas failed to raise their enthusiasm. Some were also getting their first experience of the dysentery which was to plague them for the next three months.

The bridge-builders flew to a tiny jungle airstrip where their adventures really began. Having ascertained that all the kit they'd packed in the hold was still intact despite the attentions of light-fingered locals, they piled into the back of a *collectivo*, the local form of transport, an open pick-up into which about thirty people crammed. After a three-hour journey they reached the Rio Mayo, where the entire party packed into a *peki-peki*. Three more hours, with the driver ploughing up the fast-flowing river with a maximum of two inches freeboard, brought them to a solitary hut from where they trekked another two hours up a muddy track to the little village of Rafael Belaunde, which was to be their base.

Astonished villagers gaped at the sight of such bedraggled youngsters staggering in, covered with mud from head to toe, wearily hauling their bulging rucksacks behind them. Perhaps it was not surprising that the reception was somewhat frosty: the people were convinced the Venturers were guerillas or gold-diggers at best; at worst, spies.

Next day, having got over their original shock, the villagers set to work with a will to assist the group with the building of the first bridge. The people had been relocated only recently from the region of Ayacucho, their leaders having been dragged out of church and shot by terrorists the year before. They had an incredible community spirit and in only six months had carved new homes out of dense jungle and cleared land for crops. They had not had time to become self-sufficient, however, and still depended on supplies coming up from the Rio Mayo.

This was no problem in the dry season, but in the wet season the river flooded up to twenty feet, completely cutting them off. Thus, work on the bridges was vital before the rainy season began in December. This project, more than any other, was affected by the lack of the specialist kit still held in Customs at Lima, but under the direction of a couple of stalwart British Army officers, the combined group did an incredible job, building a two-hundred-and-seventy-foot suspension bridge entirely out of local materials. The only exception to this was a thousand feet of steel wire rope, obtained in the coastal town of Chiclayo five hundred miles away, that had to be trucked to the Rio Mayo by two girl Venturers, then unwound and dragged up the jungle track by forty people.

A flourishing medical clinic was started when the bridge was finished, and by the end of the first expedition patients were arriving for medical and optical help from villages ten miles away or more. But by far the most important aspect for the Venturers was the kindness and generosity of the local people who shared what little food they had and competed in friendly but fiercely disputed football matches. Local hunters took parties of our youngsters into the jungle at night to watch wildlife.

The Tambopata party had an easier journey to their project, as in order to get to Cuzco overland they were obliged to travel south to take advantage of the few roads and railways, whilst avoiding Ayacucho, high in the Andes and noted for the activities of the violent guerilla movement *Sendero Luminosa* or 'Shining Path'. Luckily their route also went by way of some of Peru's main attractions including the Nazca Lines and Lake Titicaca.

The Tambopata Wildlife Reserve is reputedly one of the richest in South America in bird and butterfly species. Conservation projects included the study of amphibians, especially frogs and tortoises; mammal tracking; butterfly collecting; and the recording of bird species. One of their most important tasks was the work done on a worldwide project conceived by Dr Conrad Gorinsky of Bioresources. For centuries before the arrival of Western medicine, the Indians used the plant life of the forests to provide cures. Recently, scientists have discovered a plethora of medicinal substances that can only be cultivated in the fertile floor of the tropical jungle. As the jungles of the Amazon Basin are slowly being cleared by the timber companies and by 'slash and burn' agricultural techniques, Western scientists are scrambling to discover the medical potential of these areas before it is too late and the knowledge is lost forever. By working with the elders in the Indian community, Venturers endeavoured to collect the many medicinal plants they used, recording their traditional names and functions. They also dug a garden in one village with the help of school children, encouraging the people to recognise the merits of their traditional ways, and helped scientists from the Smithsonian Institute to create a Mayan garden. This was designed to introduce to the native community a system of concentrated agriculture to replace the destructive 'slash and burn' system. By combining the black soils of the swamp lands and clay from the river beds, the Mayans of Mexico had been able to make gardens with enough nutrients to sustain concentrated agriculture over long periods of time. The climate and soil features of the Peruvian jungle were similar enough for scientists to believe that the project should succeed.

In addition to these purely scientific projects, construction tasks were undertaken to increase the facilities offered to tourists and visiting researchers by the Explorers' Inn. To this end, new trails were surveyed, tree hides for canopy observation were built in the tallest trees, and water pumps were installed to provide cleaner water and reduce disease.

The projects demanded extremely hard work and dedication, especially when conducted during scorching hot days, mosquito-plagued nights, and dysentery. Adventure enough was provided by boat and jungle patrols and whitewater rafting, enlivened by fishing for the tasty piranha, and cayman counts at dead of night. Early on the morning of 4 September the Venturers got rather more adventure than they bargained for: they were woken by cries of 'Fire! Fire!' and stumbling from their tents they saw the Explorers' Inn Lodge ablaze, only three hundred yards away. By good fortune, the team leader was Reno Taini, a Californian fire-fighter, and he quickly organised a battle against the rapidly spreading flames. Unluckily, though their quick action prevented the forest from catching light, the rustic inn burned to the ground, and much scientific data stored there was lost.

The second Operation Raleigh expedition arrived in Lima on 29

September, having again suffered delays en route. Those coming from London had spent their first night away from home on Lisbon airport floor, but their lot was substantially improved on the second day in Venezuela, when they were guests of Viasa Airlines at the Macuto Sheraton in Caracas, having missed their connecting flight to Lima. Enthusiasm for sleeping bags, tents and mosquitoes waned somewhat in the face of luxury swimming pools, bars and laden restaurants, but after a week in Lima preparing kit and rations, they were keen to get on with the job.

This time, there was a choice of four project sites: Tambopata and Rio Mayo remained but now it was intended that a hovercraft ramp be built in Pucallpa, and community projects be undertaken in Peru's highest mountain region around Huaraz.

Roughly the same routes were followed to get to the project sites, but when the Pucallpa group arrived they found that their hosts, an Evangelical mission, were not after all very keen to receive them, so at the last minute another project was created and they redeployed to Rio Mayo. The journey there took four days, mainly because the bus driver appeared to delight in breaking down in the middle of river beds whilst the group watched the swirling waters rise around them. They then had to race through the middle of drug country being stopped on various occasions by army patrols, but they finally made it. They found a great reception awaiting them from the villagers, who still missed the first group. The most enthusiastic welcome came from the village store-keeper. On the departure of the first expedition she had been able to extend her little shop on the profits of the Coca-Cola drunk in preference to river water. Now she looked forward to building a supermarket!

Again, the Venturers' main task was to build a bridge, this time a two-hundred-and-ten-foot span connecting Belaunde with Paz y Esperanze. After weeks of hard labour, it was completed and looks set to last at least twenty years. The British Ambassador, HE Mr John Shakespeare, came up from Lima to open the bridge, travelling the last stretch on the back of a little pack pony whose legs were considerably shorter than his. The villagers eagerly took part in the celebrations, especially as the Venturers laid on a huge feast in their camp, entertaining all the friends they had made from outlying villages. Useful medical projects included surveying the living conditions and sanitation of the villagers, and making recommendations to reduce the two biggest causes of illness, worms and malaria. More clean water pumps were installed and the Venturers also built an adventure playground for the local children. At first the children, being unused to play, were at a loss what to do with the swings and see-saws, but once shown were so enthusiastic they are now let out of school half an hour early each day to use them.

Venturers lived on the native diet, though some preferred not to sample the local speciality – guinea-pig. Then, finally, the original expedition supplies arrived from Lima – all ten tons of them. These were greeted with rather less than enthusiasm, as everything had to be carried on foot up the track from the river to the village.

At Tambopata the scientific and exploration work continued. An eight-man boat party set off up the previously uncharted Rio D'Orbingy, and another patrol followed the Shell transect line through a hundred and forty miles of dense jungle, stumbling across three anacondas on the way. These journeys gave Venturers a taste of real adventure, of being alone and unsupported in a difficult environment. It was during this time that Pam Gaffin's team had its alarming night-time experience in the swirling river.

Approximately two weeks before the end of each expedition, the project sites were packed up and kit returned to Lima, and everyone had the opportunity to travel around Peru, whitewater rafting, climbing the 19,500 foot Misti Volcano, travelling on the world's highest railway, sailing on Lake Titicaca, flying over the famous Nazca Lines, and sampling folk music. Whilst many were energetic enough to walk the four-day Inca Trail to magnificent Machu Picchu, some preferred to sample the delights of a certain Kamikaze Bar, and nearly everyone succumbed to the charms of the Alpaca sweater sellers, the jewellery stalls and all the other 'bargains' on the streets of Cuzco, Arequipa and Lima. It was fair recompense for all their toil, and the Venturers made the most of it.

On 20 December 1985 the second expedition flew home. The six months in Peru had won Operation Raleigh some firm friends and a request to return. The Venturers had proved to many local doubters that foreign youngsters can contribute something positive to native communities in one of the world's poorest nations. Their reward had been to visit parts of a country which otherwise would have been closed to them, to meet and befriend people very different from themselves, to exchange ideas, and above all, to learn to respect their way of life. A letter written by Jane Davidson of Scotland reflects the Venturers' reactions: 'I still haven't come down to earth yet and every day finds me thinking of the country, the people and friends I made. I wish everyone I meet back here who is set in their Western ways could have come and shared my experience of the past three months. I learned so much about Peru, myself and the things that really matter in life – friendship, trust, sharing and most of all, thinking of others.'

Above: A patrol trek along the Pitisama River in the Amboro National Park, Bolivia.

Below: By contrast the environment of Chile is fantastic; Venturers made long treks across the barren Atacama Desert in the north of the country.

Opposite: Young people from a nearby village stand on the completed bridge over the Rio Mayo. Built by Venturers during the first phase in Peru, it was opened by the British Ambassador, HE John Shakespeare.

Above: Reno Tani, a volunteer firefighter from California, assists in extinguishing a tragic fire at Tambopata base camp which destroyed eight years' scientific records.

Right: Mark O'Shea, British herpatologist on the Black River expedition, with an iguana.

Overleaf: Further south in Chile a team from Operation Raleigh constructs a causeway at San Rafael glacier.

Above left: A Venturer helping in an archaeological excavation in the Atacama Desert.

Above right and below: Rowing from Melinka to San Rafael (approximately 300 miles) is tiring work. Chilean and Hong Kong Venturers prepare the evening's supper of sea urchins for their weary fellow travellers as they camp ashore on one of the tiny islands of this archipelago.

Above: Captain Bill Becker, USAF, demonstrates how light the logs are, while building an observation platform overlooking the glacier at San Rafael. Bill is a jet fighter pilot.

Right: At Laguna San Rafael, Italian Venturer Antonio Colombi abseils into a glacial crevass.

Venturers at San Rafael, Chile, erecting an observation platform (above) and manoeuvring a boat in the ice.

CHAPTER ELEVEN

Desert, Forest and Ocean

(*Chile Leader*: Major Stuart Gray, Royal New Zealand
Infantry Regiment)
(*Bolivia Leader*: Charlie King)
(*Hawaii Leader*: Lieutenant Commander John Townend VRD
Royal Navy (retired))

It was well past midnight after an exhausting day and Stuart Gray, the
New Zealand major leading our Chilean expedition, was looking forward
to a restful night's sleep. But opening his bedroom door he suddenly
sensed a presence. With a swift movement he flicked on the lights and
stared in amazement: on his bed lay a frightened young girl quite clearly
in the final stages of labour. How she had got into the house or who she
was he had no idea.

Being the father of three and well-rehearsed in the procedure, he
quickly summoned an ambulance and accompanied the lady to hospital
where, at 4.30 am, she gave birth to a five-pound baby girl. The hospital
staff, presuming Stuart to be the father, offered their congratulations
and a form to fill out in Spanish. Realising he was being asked to accept
total responsibility, Stuart completed it as best he could, but against
'Father's Name' he generously wrote 'Charlie Daniel' and left hurriedly.
He had been in the country long enough to know that such incidents are
best accepted without question – in Chile anything can happen and
often does.

I remembered the graphic descriptions of our recce section who had
gone out to Chile months earlier to liaise with local representatives, set
up projects and organise support. It had been a long hard day of negotiations and Malcolm Hyatt, our International Division Director, knew
he and geologist John Pethwick had earned a stiff drink; but now, on
leaving the bar, he was surprised at its effect. The pavement had become

a moving air bed and most people in the street looked correspondingly wonky. Within seconds, however, everyone around them was running, and he realised that what was amiss might not be entirely attributable to the pisco sours.

'Get clear of the buildings,' he yelled, and as coping stones crashed onto the cobbles, both men fled, quite literally, for their lives, into the open plaza. All around was an awful rumbling and tinkling of breaking glass punctuated by screams of the Chilean women who had experienced the terror of an earthquake before.

It was soon over and they wearily made their way back to the hotel. Terrified guests were booking out as they walked through the lobby, but there seemed no point in leaving: it's said that no shell ever lands in the same place twice. Wondering if the shower would still be working, Malcolm opened the door of his room and was mildly amused to find that the ceiling had fallen on his bed and all his belongings were buried under half a ton of plaster.

'Oh well,' he thought, 'just another typical Op Raleigh day.'

Originally I'd planned only three expeditions in Chile but after seeing the excellent opportunities open to us amid the mountains and fjords of the south, this was extended to four. Due to the severity of the southern winter, our first three-month expedition was to take place in Chile's northern regions, an area which surely must rank among the world's wonders. Soaring volcanoes, stark lava fields and huge, rolling dunes make a startling contrast to a seemingly endless desert. The immense Atacama runs for over six hundred miles, with many vast areas where it has never rained in recorded history.

Alas, our first Chilean phase threatened to begin badly. Many of the proposed projects never materialised or fell through only days before the expedition's arrival. Perhaps the Chilean committee had expected too much of us, coming, as they saw it, from a host of relatively wealthy nations. Perhaps the effects of the earthquake had still to be reckoned with. There were other problems. The country is divided into twelve regions, each virtually self-governing, and we soon discovered that arrangements made in Santiago are not always effective fifteen hundred miles away. Planning ahead in South American countries doesn't always ensure the end result, and we were confronted daily with what came to be called the 'South American factor'.

Thankfully the problem of our tasks was solved by CONAF, the national park organisation, who, having a surfeit of work and a very tight budget, welcomed our offer of labour with open arms and stepped in at the last moment with new projects throughout Chile. Our expedition extended for almost a thousand miles, covering sixteen project sites, and the barren, almost uninhabited, northern wasteland made the distances seem even greater. Furthermore, to the discomfort of several Venturers who'd brought clothes designed for perhaps more predictable desert weather – the Atacama was freezing cold.

By now *Sir Walter Raleigh* was anchored off the small port of Mejillones, with a mixed crew of British Army, Portuguese, and US Navy personnel, plus our splendid Hull-based merchant seamen. Wide beaches and spectacular rock formations stretched along a coast which reverberated to the roar of explosions as the local dynamite factory tested its wares. Oddly, these blasts seemed to have no effect on the pelicans whirling sleepily, endlessly above the ship in the clear cold air. Fat sealions barked at our divers, seeming to invite them in for a swim, so they were delighted when we started on an oceanographic survey of the bay, clearly under the impression that the supply of human playmates had been laid on for their benefit.

At this time Raleigh's finances were at a low ebb. In setting up the Operation we had taken bids from all countries wishing to participate. For example, Australia had asked to send two hundred and forty Venturers, Oman a hundred and the United States committees, not unreasonably, had said they would like to bid for fifteen hundred. Now, eight months into the venture, it was a different story. For a wide variety of perfectly understandable reasons, many of our national committees had not been able to fill their quotas, and although our expenditure was well within budget our income was falling far behind. Every possible measure had been taken to bridge the gap and we had raised Britain's quota from three hundred and seventy-five per year to six hundred and sixty in the first twelve months. But there is only so much cash in the dear old UK and we simply could not generate any more funded

Venturers from home. Then again, after eight months of continuous seaborne operation, the flagship desperately needed maintenance, and there were all the annual insurance surveys to be done. Help was at hand. David Allfrey discovered a place to moor the ship free of charge at the picturesque little city of Puerto Montt in southern Chile. There, thanks to the generosity of a Mr Kochifas, we could anchor within a hundred feet of the shore using his buoys, and obtain all the facilities necessary for the refit at low cost – it seemed too good to be true.

If we ditched our original plan to go to the Falklands we could stop at Puerto Montt, be close enough to provide support for the forthcoming expeditions in the south, and refit the ship in preparation for her voyage across the Pacific in 1986. We decided to do just that. Tac HQ, however, had to operate from somewhere. Puerto Montt would be too far from our people in Bolivia and Peru, not to mention Hawaii, so we opted to go ashore at nearby Antofagasta, the great city of the north and gateway to the world's richest copper mining area. Kind Chileans found us an office in a government building and, moving our fifteen HQ staff into a large rented house totally devoid of furniture, we set up shop on land, and *Sir Walter Raleigh* sailed on for Puerto Montt.

Stuart Gray had set up his own expedition HQ in some old Ferro Carril Antofagasta-Bolivia railway company huts at Mejillones. His most northerly project was situated at Lago Chungara, one of the world's highest lakes at 15,800 feet. Though surrounded by barren desert, the lakeshore abounds with wildlife: deer roam freely, long-eared rabbits (*Viscacha*) bask undisturbed in the sunshine, and graceful pink flamingoes congregate on the still blue waters. Around the CONAF hut in which the team lived, proud domestic llamas and alpacas wandered nonchalantly, their brightly coloured headgear and tinkling bells giving them, to us, a faintly ridiculous appearance.

Towering above the camp was the mighty Parinacota Volcano, its snow-covered peak a permanent challenge to the Venturers.

'We can't leave here without climbing it,' proclaimed Welshman Hamish Osborne, gazing in awe at the glimmering slopes. Soon, all attention focused on the hope of reaching the lofty summit. The only real problem was a lack of climbing kit: we had not come to Chile expecting to assault mountains. Fortunately Martin Fitzgerald, quarter-master aboard ship, located a few ropes, carabiners, slings and some old crampons, and using these and borrowed ice axes, the group set out. Though Parinacota might not compare with Everest, it was certainly far higher and more challenging than anything they'd ever tackled before, but after a prolonged struggle, three teams reached the top of northern Chile's highest peak, and were rewarded with unparalleled views along the length of the Andes. The descent, seen through binoculars from the camp, looked equally dramatic. The glazed ice was perfect for sliding, so the leading group celebrated their victory by sledging down the mountain on their behinds – much to the detriment of their breeches.

Further south, the desert region provided an opportunity for a wide range of archaeological projects. The arid conditions are perfect for the preservation of ancient artefacts, and the fact that most of the desert is now uninhabited means that many of these relics have lain undisturbed for centuries. On the coast, at Camerones, Chilean archaeologist Professor Hans Niemeyer (Conservador de Museo Nacional de Historia Natural) oversaw eight excavations of pre-Columbian sites, one by each of the Venturers in the team. The work was dirty and hard, but they enjoyed it.

Although in the end it proved immensely successful, the project had a difficult start. David Allfrey's Scottish soldiers had previously visited the area to deposit the necessary rations and equipment. Speaking Spanish in thick Glaswegian accents, they had left strict instructions with the mayor and a local café owner, in whose store they left everything, that 'on pain of death' they were not to mention to *anyone* the whereabouts of the kit – except, of course, to people like themselves.

Three weeks later the Camerones group, under the leadership of an Australian Army officer, Captain Simon Harvey, arrived to begin their project and collect the stores. Despite enquiries in best Sydney Spanish, no one in the village would admit to any knowledge of them.

Not surprisingly, frantic messages flashed across Chile and, believing that everything had been stolen, I contacted the Intendente; the regional commander, for help. Troops were despatched forthwith, police ordered to investigate, and the entire village was subjected to a veritable inquisition. At last the stores were discovered, exactly where the recce team had left them.

'*Se Escosia* say we are to tell no one,' explained the perplexed mayor, 'except people like them – and they were very fierce men.'

The Venturers, camped six miles away on the coast, had spent three days without rations, living on such crabs, clams and octopus as they could catch. Yet despite their discomfort, they could still see the funny side of things.

Many centuries ago the remote desert oasis of San Pedro de Atacama had been the centre of a flourishing Paleolithic civilization based within impressive rock fortresses built upon the steep mountains that almost encircle the green valley. Thousands of ancient graves scattered throughout the hills are now beginning to yield their secrets. An extraordinary museum, set up by the late Father Gustave Le Paige, contains numerous mummies, skulls, stone-age tools, jewellery, weapons and wood carvings. The mummies, many with their hair intact, were found still clad in their fine burial clothes.

A large group of Venturers, directed by local archaeologists, helped with the excavations, and in fifteen days recovered twenty-nine pre-Columbian mummies, many perfectly preserved. It was fascinating work. Discoveries included the graves of important warriors, buried with their weapons and a llama, presumably as food for the afterlife. Some men carried a pouch of drug-taking implements on their belts! One of the most extraordinary finds was made by Mary Jane Hinchcliffe, a trainee schoolteacher, and Nicola Kearney, a young Irish girl. They unearthed a large basket containing an earthenware pot which, when opened, was found to contain a cake at least fifteen hundred years old.

San Pedro proved to be a favourite site. Though tiny, it had much to offer: archaeology, community work at the local orphanage, adventure, desert survival and, of course, the hot spring swimming pool! Everyone had an opportunity to become involved with the extremely hospitable local people and gained a very special insight into Chilean culture.

Near the former nitrate mining centre of Marie Elena one project was set up which combined archaeology with desert exploration; a challenge in survival and logistics. Teams set out in vehicles to follow the Llama Trail, an ancient trading route, from the coast across the desert into Bolivia. The Atacama area had once been Bolivian territory and supported many nitrate towns, but these were abandoned and wooded areas destroyed during the War of the Pacific (1879–83) in which Bolivia and Peru fought Chile. Only two remain out of three hundred communities.

Somewhere, out in the dusty desert, up to three hundred sweet water wells existed, but all maps showing their location had been lost in the war. If Operation Raleigh could find these wells, cultivation and re-population of this wilderness might become a reality.

The instigator of this ambitious venture was Victor Hugo Vega Zapeda, Co-ordinator of the Community Development Plan in Marie Elena, who had learned English especially to be able to converse with us. Victor believed strongly in the potential of the desert and his enthusiasm was infectious: everyone involved was inspired by the aims of the project and its implications for the future. A large area of desert was explored and eventually two lost towns were discovered, their outlines just visible above the surface of the sand; it will take local archaeologists ten years to excavate them fully. Much more important, however, their two wells were also located. Victor Hugo was ecstatic!

Meanwhile, back in Antofagasta, so many Chilean youngsters had demonstrated a desire to join us that we decided to hold a local selection weekend. Although organised along similar lines to those held elsewhere, some allowances had to be made. Chilean youngsters had very little experience of outdoor pursuits and at first they were totally unprepared for the constant pressure that a selection weekend exerts on both mind and body. In Chile, life is taken at a slow pace: why make things difficult for yourself? But as the weekend progressed the young Chileans proved themselves and even began to enjoy the outlandish situation. One youngster who badly sliced his hand while preparing supper was quite adamant that he did not want to leave his group to visit the local hospital, so the Tac HQ doctor, John Davies, used the back of our Land Rover as a surgery, and proceeded to stitch him up. With a well bandaged hand and a determined smile, the lad continued the weekend and was eventually successful in being selected. A disabled girl was an inspiration to us all. She had lost a leg through cancer, yet attempted everything with such determination that at times she left the others behind.

Despite the fact that many of the science projects never materialized, those which did proved very successful. Among these was a study of raised beaches sponsored by King's College, London. A young, bearded graduate, Mark Woodgate, led the project assisted by Christine Hudson, a British surveyor, and nine Venturers. They were investigating the rate at which the Andes are rising and pulling the shoreline up with them. As the Pacific plates moved beneath the continental shelf, they effectively created a series of stepped beaches, pushing them upwards and backwards from the ocean. By measuring the height of these 'cliffs' and using carbon dating on fossils found along them, it is possible to determine the date at which each was formed, and thus to establish the rate and frequency of such tectonic movements. The data will be used to study the incidence of earthquakes in this region, and possibly even to predict when they are most likely to occur. Mark, anticipating that six weeks constant surveying might become tedious and not provide enough adventure to stretch the Venturers, planned a desert trek between the two main survey sites.

What a strange sight the group must have looked trailing along the main road just outside Antofagasta. *Gringos* aren't a common sight, but when you encounter twelve young people dressed in distinctive Venturer style, stretched out at varying points along the route and either bending over, crouching or lying on the ground, curiosity is inevitably aroused. There was, of course, a simple explanation for their gymnastics – goat's cheese! The group had purchased some rather delicious-looking soft white cheese for lunch, and now all those who had partaken of the delicacy were being violently sick.

Back at the Mejillones base HQ an urgent message had been relayed; it read 'Eight Venturers in hospital due to intoxication.' There was an awful half-hour of waiting, during which we envisaged the probable headlines: 'Raleigh Venturers found drunk and disorderly!' So it was with relief that we learned that the intoxication referred to food and not alcohol poisoning. Luckily it was only a mild form, but to show their concern the local doctors, singling out Jane Mulroy from Rotherham as the worst case, administered upon her a whopping great injection which would probably have cured malaria, typhoid and cholera all at once! The *Carabineros* (Chilean police) then raided the local shops and confiscated the illegal goats' cheese, which had been made from untreated milk possessing a dangerously high bacteria content.

Once recovered, the group set off on the first of their desert treks, covering ninety miles. Sergeant Tom Bartridge, USAF, ran very successful desert survival courses where Venturers spent six days with only minimum food and water, learning to keep alive. They were presented with a live rabbit to kill, and surprisingly the girls showed themselves to be the least squeamish of the lot about this. The Venturers had prepared their own caches of food and water which were placed along the route, but it soon became apparent that the food content was inadequate. They stomped on, averaging fifteen miles a day, through countryside that was hot and arid with no vegetation. When the terrain grew mountainous, they were plagued by boiling hot days and freezing temperatures once the sun set. At night they bivvied down in hollows, caves or sometimes dilapidated shacks, remnants of the mining era.

Without exception the discussion of food dominated each and every conversation, at first playfully but, once the hunger pangs began in earnest, it became a serious matter. They remember vividly the terrible cache which contained only one tin of baked beans to share for breakfast, and not much more for lunch and supper. Morale was very low at times, but when they marched into Hornitos, a small coastal resort, looking very dusty, thin and hungry, they were proud to have reached their destination. They had never at any time been in real danger since there were adequate supplies of water and a radio watch was kept: but we decided, in this as in other situations, that they would learn far better from their own mistakes. In the event the trek stretched the group both mentally and physically, and created a very strong and lasting bond between them. However, despite female Venturers' delight at the amount of weight lost, they ensured that on the next patrol the caches were packed with more than enough food.

A community project in Santiago brought the northern Chile phase to a most successful conclusion. A group of thirteen Venturers from the various project sites volunteered to help rebuild a centre for handicapped children which had been severely damaged in the recent earthquake. Their work was greatly appreciated and achieved some excellent news coverage. It also attracted the attention of Madam Pinochet, wife of the President, and this helped us to overcome a great amount of red tape in the future.

Although the Chilean bureaucracy was finally coming round to our side, in Bolivia the system was definitely working against us, which added an extra measure of suspense to each adventure.

In the gloomy Amboro Forest a twig snapped, and Charlie froze, but after a moment's hesitation he started on again. The jungle was thick here, and with each step forward he searched the underbush in front of him. For what, he wasn't quite sure: a man with a gun, perhaps, or a crowd of local farmers armed with machetes, waiting . . .

As he pushed his way through the tangled groundcover, the bespectacled manager of Crawley Job Centre whom I'd asked to lead the Bolivia expedition wondered to himself why he had ever agreed to take it on. It had seemed so simple back in Crawley, it had still seemed simple in the sunlight and safety of nearby Capriconia Ranch, although the local *campansinos*, engaged in a running political battle with the new Government, had threatened to shoot any *gringo* setting foot in the Amboro. After almost a month of waiting, unable to get in to their designated project sites, calling the farmers' bluff had seemed the only logical alternative. Now, deep in the jungle with thirty-four Venturers and staff behind him and God only knows what in front, it seemed an altogether different story. A challenge, someone had called it, probably me. Real adventure book stuff. The only problem was that the books never seemed to mention the fear, the cold hollowness that grips at your insides. Leaves rustled and a wide-eyed kinkajou scurried for cover at the big man's approach. Charlie breathed a sigh of relief.

They never did encounter the resistance they had expected. The *campansinos*, though they met our group's incursion with initial hostility and suspicion, failed to carry out their threats. With time, the expedition even became welcome in the area, primarily due to the hard work put in at the village clinic by nurses Jan Hawke, Anne Sewell and their able assistant Marcella Taylor.

Trouble, when it came, came from quite a different quarter. One day, while out on patrol, a team suddenly found themselves surrounded by a squad of Bolivian soldiers armed with automatic rifles. They had unknowingly stumbled into a sensitive military area and were held for eight hours before US Marine Corps First Lieutenant Bob Bray could persuade their captors that they were neither mercenaries nor spies.

Back at Capriconia, the ranch owned by Norwegians Sven and Elli Scheen, the group had been struggling with a similar paramilitary image. Inhabitants of the nearby village of San Pedro were convinced that Operation Raleigh Venturers were in reality a crack US Army unit stationed in the area just in case the July elections went the 'wrong' way. Here as well, suspicions were diffused by the mercy work of Jan and Anne who treated a total of eight hundred villagers suffering from malnutrition, parasites, skin diseases and other minor ailments, and by the installation of a village irrigation system undertaken by David Swinbourne and his team.

While Charlie King and his administrative staff scurried back and forth along the muddied roads to Santa Cruz in an attempt to get Government permission to enter the Amboro, expedition scientists made the best of their time at Capriconia. Barry Walker, a British ornithologist living in Peru, directed the Venturers in undertaking a local bird survey which succeeded in identifying a total of one hundred and eighty-six species.

Once in the park, the group was able to start on its main scientific projects. Two camps were set up, each at differing altitudes, to test the effect of elevation on the local environment. The high camp, as it came to be called, was established twelve miles up the Rio Pitisami amid dense primary forest edging a massive gorge. The low camp was set up in the Rio Saquayo basin, on a wide sandy bank flanked on one side by low forest and on the other by a high cliff. From here scientists from New Mexico University conducted a small mammals project; assistant Venturers encountered racoons, sloths, rats, and discovered what may possibly prove to be a new species of bat. A mouse racoon, twice the size of any of its kind previously noted in the area, was also observed near the camp, and there were sightings of animals moving up from the Amazon basin, many of which had never been seen in the Amboro before. Continuing his bird survey here, Barry noted an additional four hundred and seventy-two species, many of which, like the mammals, were making their first recorded appearance at Amboro. A butterfly project undertaken by Jonathon Ash and Liza Johnson succeeded in the collection of three hundred species, many of which proved to be quite rare.

Science was not, however, the only thing that occupied the Venturers' time in Amboro. Members of the Bolivian Andean Club volunteered their time to hold a week-long theoretical course on survival followed by seven days in the jungle, during which Venturers found themselves dining on termites, snails, rats, and snakes and extracting their liquid refreshment from vines. One of the expedition's highlights proved to be the assault on Cerro Amboro. After several unsuccessful attempts, Venturers Dave Powell, Dave Swinbourne and Stefan Schaefer fought their way to the top, becoming the first Europeans to reach its summit.

During their stay in Bolivia, each of the Venturers enjoyed the status of millionaire as inflation dropped the value of the peso to 1,500,000 to the dollar. One youngster was given the chance of gaining even more wealth when, while waiting at the airport for a homebound flight, he was offered £50,000 to smuggle a briefcase full of cocaine into the States. He politely declined.

While our Bolivian expedition was chasing butterflies and feasting on the jungle's culinary delights, a group of seaborne Venturers was crossing the Pacific aboard *Zebu*. They had left Panama in early July and after a four-day stopover in the Galapagos taking on fuel and water, and exploring the islands with naturalists from the Charles Darwin Research Station, they had set off on the long haul to Hawaii. It was on the morning of 19 August 1985, after twenty-nine days of tradewinds and squalls, that these by now seasoned sailors caught their first glimpse of the snow-crowned peak of Mauna Kea.

Even as *Zebu* stood off Hilo roads, another crew of Venturers was toiling away on the slopes of a nearby volcano. These youngsters, under expedition leader John Townend, had come to work with the staff of the Hawaii Volcanoes National Park on conservation projects. The area contains a vast range of ecosystems, from mist forests to lava deserts. In recent years, however, Hawaii's fragile habitats have been threatened by the introduction of foreign species, hearty strangers who have slowly taken over from the more fragile Island forms, long protected by their isolation. The plants and animals of Volcanoes National Park are unique to Hawaii and people threw themselves into the task of ensuring their preservation. They hunted and captured wild pigs and goats whose voracious appetites have ravaged the native rainforests; built fences to keep them out of the Park area; dug up and otherwise eradicated non-native plant species, such as kahili ginger, strawberry guave, Russian olive and banana poka; and helped in the radio-tracking of the rare and and endangered Hawaiian goose, the nene. In a letter to the Superintendent of the park, management ecologist Dan Taylor wrote of the Venturers' endeavours:

'We must consider the service project a remarkable success. Urgently needed work in vegetation and wildlife management programs was accomplished. It will now be possible for our staff to maintain control of these areas. Venturers' attitudes towards work, their sense of responsibility, willingness to accept challenges and risks, and their bearing of dignity and worth were excellent models for our staff who worked with them.'

Mr Taylor estimated that our work in Hawaii Volcanoes had saved the park over £21,000, a sum they could ill afford, for a job that very much needed doing.

In addition to helping preserve the local environment, the Venturers spent time immersed in the traditional Hawaiian way of life. Working with and learning from Rangers at Hoonaunau City of Refuge National Park, our young men and women came to know which trees and plants provided medicines and raw materials for the ancient people of the Islands. They tried their hands at outrigger canoe building and sailing, learned to weave baskets of coconut fronds, catch fish with graceful throw nets and eat *poi* with their fingers. On one occasion when he visited the site, John Townend even found his Venturers dressed in traditional Hawaiian garments: 'The girls looked most demure and noticeably more attractive than they did in their usual gear, and the men, bronzed by their work out of doors, looked the part; that is until they turned around: the white cheeks of their bottoms normally covered by shorts made them look like pandas from behind.'

The Venturers ended their stay on the Islands by paying a visit to the Bay of Kealakekua on the south west coast of Hawaii, continuing in the tradition of all passing British ships by cleaning the monument commemorating the death of an earlier visitor to the Islands, Captain James Cook.

CHAPTER TWELVE

To the Ends of the Earth

(*Chile Leader*: Major Stuart Gray, Royal New Zealand Infantry
Regiment
Major Mark Bentinck, late Royal Marines)

Chilean lakeland is one of the least spoilt places on earth. Stretching for
hundreds of miles, scores of emerald lakes glitter amidst beautiful
mountains. This is a land of snow-capped volcanoes, deep woodland
meadows and small peaceful villages. There are flowers by the acre,
great pine forests and awe-inspiring waterfalls.

Puerto Montt, capital of the region, lies on a flat plain beside Relon-
cavi Bay, overlooked by the perfect cone of the Orsono Volcano. Here
Sir Walter Raleigh lay at anchor, already swarming with eager Chilean
workers, hammering, scraping, painting and welding. Paul Bernard,
our Spanish-speaking purser, had found us a small house in town and
thanks to the kindness of our agents, Empremar, we were given the use
of an office. It was still winter, and the wind and rain swept down from
the Andes as Tac HQ moved into these new quarters. With his indomitable vigour, Chris Eley soon had the radios working and Peta's type-
writer began pounding out the usual scores of letters to sponsors,
organisers and Venturers that I have to write to wherever I am. A new
contingent of American servicemen arrived under the highly efficient
and humorous Captain Don Gassman USAF, who was to be my
adjutant; and our second Chilean expedition got under way.

Stuart Gray's HQ was now a further four hundred miles south at
the sprawling frontier city of Coyhaique, capital of Chile's eleventh
and least known region. Referred to locally as the 'End of the Earth',
the wild, untamed beauty of Chile's Austral zone is breathtaking, a
rugged extravagance of nature. Blue glaciers, mirror-black lakes,
snowfields, ragged rows of mountain ranges and volcanocs join a

seemingly endless coast of bays, channels, inlets, fjords and islands.

Flying high above this splendid wilderness one sees few traces of man. A lone track, perhaps, and maybe an isolated Indian hut or fishing village. This is real frontier country as the American West must once have been. Over a third of all Chile lies here, yet this immense wilderness holds less than 3% of its population. The incredible terrain, the weather and the miles of uninhabited land offered us wonderful opportunity for adventure.

Situated at the northern tip of the Patagonian Icefield, the massive glacier of San Rafael, isolated and wild, provided an awesome setting for one of our southerly projects. The only building amidst this wilderness is an abandoned hotel offering a spectacular view of the glacier: left empty by the lack of visitors, it became one of our more luxurious bases.

It was not long before the Venturers discovered that the quiet beauty which surrounded them also concealed many dangers. The project leader, USAF Captain Bill Becker, more like a burly Father Christmas with his twinkling eyes and large beard than the fighter pilot he is, recalls one incident out on the ice. Behind his laughter, however, one realised only too well how close tragedy had been.

A team of four – Bill, Miles Cohen (an American Operation Drake Young Explorer) and two British Venturers, Kit and Des – set out in one of the local wooden boats to haul lumber from the dock near the hotel to the base of the glacier; from there it would be manhandled up the mountain and used to construct an observation platform. The alternative trek overland, through difficult hilly terrain, would have taken weeks. As Bill tells it:

'We'd been waiting for two days but the ice had been so thick we couldn't get through. Finally, one night, I just said "OK guys, tomorrow, no matter what, we're going." What a mistake that was.

'The next morning the westerly winds were pushing the ice in so that none of it was melting: the bay was the world's largest slush daquiri. It was so thick we were able to walk on it, dragging the boat through the ice. We had been out about three hours before we finally broke through the flows and reached a narrow strip of clear water just in front of the glacier. I glanced over the gunwale. All the paint was gone from the bottom and there were large scars where the ice had taken chunks out of the wood. I just shook my head. With the boat alongside the jagged cliff face we started to unload the timber.

'We'd almost managed to get two of the largest logs halfway off when a skyscraper-size chunk of ice broke from the hundred-and-fifty-foot high glacier-face, and came crashing down like an apartment block into the lagoon only a hundred yards away! We had about ten seconds to get the logs off before the first fifteen-foot wave struck us, carrying the boat straight up the cliff-face, then dragging it back down to the rocks again. That, however, was just one of the small outrider waves being pushed ahead by a monster surge still coming at us! Self-preservation took over. Again we were hurled upwards and as the little craft was at its highest point I took a seven-foot leap and clung on to the cliff like Spiderman. Luckily my jump pushed the boat backwards, preventing it from crashing into the rocks once again on the way down.

'Meanwhile Des had started up the engine in an effort to head out and ride the next wave. He was too late. Again they were swept up the face. As the boat dropped back this time, the propellor struck the ice and flipped the motor upwards into the boat, ripping away half the transom. Des was momentarily hypnotised by the spinning blade, only inches from his face, but he managed to collect himself and cut the motor. Kit, in the bow, stood in a complete daze, unable to comprehend what was happening.

'At last the shock waves subsided, but then the craft, almost filled with freezing water, was slowly being dragged out by the current into the lagoon. Somehow I managed to fling a line across to Mark, reaching him with only inches to spare. We hauled the boat in and two petrified, near-frozen Venturers stepped ashore – glad to feel firm ground beneath their feet.'

The most difficult part of the whole episode, Bill said later, was trying to explain what had happened, through an interpreter, to the boat's Chilean owner.

Elsewhere in Chile, we built bridges and huts and two groups surveyed tracks through dense forest, using horses to carry stones. Swollen rivers, broken terrain and dense forest made progress so slow that their rations ran dangerously low. Obligingly, one or the horses died, so they ate it.

At Puerto Montt, Di Rosenthal helped the municipality by organising a diving team to carry out an oceanographic survey. As ever, Merseyside's excellent landing craft proved invaluable and in spite of the water temperature (around 12 decrees C), a useful scientific task was completed.

To my surprise CONAF produced some 'unexplored territory' for us only thirty miles from Puerto Montt. It was an area of dense forest, mountains and lakes known as the Alerce Andino. Former Park warden and now US Navy medical corpsman Jim Bozeman likened it to a mixture of the Panama jungle and the bamboo forests of Japan, with Antarctic temperatures thrown in. He led a patrol of Venturers to hack out new trails in an area where no one had ever been. The waist-deep mud, tenacious leeches, torrential rain and hail were quite a challenge; and the spoor of large puma seen near the camp in the mornings helped to keep people on their toes.

In December our friend Dr Harry Brown arrived with his SEE International opthalmic team to operate on cataract victims. Thanks to Charlie Daniel's excellent work in Santiago, the Customs passed through the nineteen boxes of medical equipment without comment and within a few days the team were hard at work in the expedition area. With co-operation from a local Chilean opthalmic surgeon and assisted by Venturers, Harry and his colleagues set about their sight-restoring mission. In four days of intensive surgery, often working for sixteen hours at a stretch, they gave back sight to seventeen people and provided hundreds of pairs of free spectacles to poor people who would never normally have such a service.

There were some strange incidents. One ninety-year-old gentleman was led back to bed after his cataract operation by an attractive American Venturer, Linda Walters. As soon as he was between the sheets he muttered something, leapt up, grabbed Linda and gave her a smacking great kiss. Not understanding Spanish, she asked someone who did whether he was trying to express his thanks for the operation.

'Oh no,' said a Chilean nurse, 'he just likes pretty girls and now he can see them again.' Another elderly patient, a lady examined by Harry's wife Baillie, was found to be wearing spectacles fitted with plain glass. She cheerfully confessed they did her no good – she wore them for the trend!

It was a rewarding feeling to be part of such a humane project, which gave so marvellous a Christmas present to the people in this remote area.

As the year drew to a close Major Mark Bentinck, a lean, quiet-spoken ex-Royal Marine, arrived to take over from Stuart Gray. A new expedition would fly to Chile in January and yet another in March, and Mark had numerous testing projects planned for them.

Across the ocean *Zebu* had completed the last leg of her Pacific crossing and sailed majestically into Sydney harbour. In Canberra, Robin Letts was putting the finishing touches on the plans for the four massive Australian phases, whilst the New Zealand committee were paving the way for an exciting programme in a land not dissimilar to southern Chile. Our teams for the Solomons, Indonesia, and Papua New Guinea were making final preparations, and in Peking Henry Day and Richard Snailham were negotiating with the Chinese over our 1987 visit to Tibet.

My good friend Maurice Taylor had become chairman of our United States committee and the tireless Mark Bensen was striving to increase the number of American Venturers. In Britain, Roberta Howlett was driving on her Venturer selection team to greater heights. We all knew that the financial success of Operation Raleigh depended on obtaining more international Venturers, and I had felt especially frustrated by being unable to use our marvellous flagship, laid up for refits, in support of this drive.

It was clear that whilst we were winning the battle at the front, we urgently needed support at the rear, and so I decided that Charlie Daniel and I should return to Britain and spend the first part of 1986 supporting our overworked CHQ.

On a boiling hot Christmas Day the Venturers of the second Chilean expedition poured on to the flagship for a momentous party. Fit, happy and confident, with new-found friends and a host of tales to tell, they'd soon be on their way home. With the day drawing to a close an American pastor joined me in conducting a carol service on deck. We took the theme of peace on earth and said Sir Francis Drake's Prayer:

O Lord God, when thou givest to thy servants to endeavour

any great matter, grant us to know that it is not the beginning but the continuing of the same unto the end, until it be thoroughly finished, which yieldeth the true glory: through him who for the finishing of thy work laid down his life, our Redeemer Jesus Christ. Amen.

As the last carol died away across the sunlit blue waters of the sound, I was reminded that this was just the end of Operation Raleigh's beginning. There were still three years to run and many, many more young people round the world to take up the challenge.

ACKNOWLEDGEMENTS

I must record special indebtedness to various members of
Operation Raleigh's team of organisers for their continuing
work on our behalf:

David Barton, former RAF officer and our senior accountant,
of Ernst and Whinney; and the well-known law firm, Birbeck
Montague, who generously agreed to become our legal advisers.
Almost everything that Operation Raleigh did would have
some legal implication: all important documentation from the
application forms for Venturers to the contracts relating to ships
must comply with the law. Consequently, Ron Murrell, who
looked after our legal interests, was hardly to have a day go by
without doing something for us. He never dreamt he would
become so involved; after all, David King had simply asked if
he'd do a little job for a charity. Luckily Ron had an adventurous
spark in his nature.

Dr Stephen Sutton, a leading scientist who had been with us
on Drake, kindly agreed to spearhead the scientific research
programme from his desk at Leeds University. We also re-
cruited a young botanist, Caroline Ash, to assist in the coordination of the research projects. I don't know how we would
have survived without the enormous help of Maurice Taylor
who did so much to promote the Operation Raleigh films and
raise funds.

On the PR front we needed a massive team, and Beth
Barrington-Haynes, who had done such a magnificent job for
Drake, came along to help us voluntarily. My good friend Anna
Cooke, who had taught me a great deal about appearances on
TV, lent a hand and Richard Snailham, our researcher, saw
that we were well supplied with historical facts. It was not easy
to find a PR Director, but eventually Dr Andrew Sinclair
volunteered for the post, although he admitted he was really a
historian and novelist rather than an expert on Fleet Street.
He introduced a wonderful Canadian lady, Jennifer Watts,
who eventually became a leading material procurer for us.

Frances Chiddell, long-standing editor of Scientific Exploration Society's newsletter, kindly agreed to run Operation
Raleigh News as well. Much of our promotion was channelled

through the medium of lectures and after-dinner talks, ably arranged by Dabber and Paddy Davies of Associated Speakers, and also by my old friend Barbara Snell.

Through Michael and Phyliss Angliss, we obtained much help from Rotary, and Phyliss did a marvellous job with our souvenirs. I had already been joined by TA Major Wandy Swales as 'Chief of Staff' and his pleasant and friendly attitude did much to attract people to Raleigh. I was extremely fortunate, after the sad death of our mountaineering expert, Christopher Davies, to inherit the lady who had become his assistant. Sue Farrington became a good friend and a close adviser; her varied career had included much travel and a spell in the Diplomatic Service, which was to prove invaluable.

Although I had made many suggestions to Chris Sainsbury that he should give up this life of adventure and settle down to a steady career in fine arts, I couldn't shake him off. With me since 1976, he has remained one of the most loyal and hard-working members of the team. Chris is a real expert on most things photographic and has a fine eye for a picture. He became our Audio Visual Coordinator, doing virtually the same job he had done on Drake.

I was very fortunate to find a former army colleague and old expedition buddy Roger Chapman looking for a job, and I brought him in to head up the awesome task of selecting the young people. There were literally hundreds of others who helped, many of whom joined our permanent team. The cry was always money, money, money, and we were most fortunate to have the backing of a number of Government Ministers and also the Manpower Services Commission. The Foreign and Commonwealth Office could not have been more helpful, and in the private sector that splendid organisation, the St George's Day Club, gave us considerable assistance, thanks to the efforts of Bart Bartholomew.

Each county in Britain was to have its own representative and many old friends rallied to the cause. There was Vic Rudge, a renowned charity worker, who took over Hampshire, and a highly motivated schoolmaster, Mervyn Evans, who agreed to run Gloucester. At a late night party Brigadier Sydney Robertson, a marvellous character and retired gunner, was persuaded to become chairman of the Orkneys. An army sailing chum, John Cuthill, took on Cornwall once again, whilst a splendid newcomer who had long worked in Scouting, Wilkie Burdon, agreed to run an area in Wales. Another dedicated enthusiast,

Major Arthur Rose, seized the challenging Merseyside region for us and former Royal Marine Mike Gambier took on Somerset. Through the help of a beautiful and charming American lady, Ann Tweedy, we established a network in the Scottish Highlands. Ann owns one of the most lovely castles I have ever seen and this gave us a splendid base to recruit supporters' help. All these folk knew that they were giving a pledge in a worthwhile cause and their combined contribution was simply enormous.

At Buckingham Palace Michael Colborne, Secretary to the Prince of Wales, had become our official link. A marvellous man and a former Fleet Chief Petty Officer in the Royal Navy, he had a high degree of tact and persuasion. Michael's advice and good counsel will be of lasting benefit.

Working from a Whitehall basement, we commenced our search for the ships and were lucky to have the support of the Shipwrights Company. They provided a naval architect, John Hind, to assist, and with the help of Shipbrokers Messrs Clarksons of London and a specification drawn up by Captain Mike Kichenside, former skipper of *Eye of the Wind*, the quest began.

Whilst all this was going on in Britain, new organisations were springing up overseas. Sir Gordon White, former Chairman of Operation Drake in America, came to our aid in setting up an embryo organisation in New York, and in Miami expedtionner and diver David Pincus gave us the backing of the Underwater Society, of which he was Secretary.

The liaison and reconnaissance teams that toured the world on our behalf did sterling work. David King and I visited Hong Kong and Australia. London banker and ex-Naval Officer John Groves spent many days in North America whilst retired businessman and ex-Sapper officer Anetoli Vassilissin concentrated on South America. General Sir John Mogg and I visited Oman where the Deputy Prime Minister himself had promised significant support, and I also visited Honduras with Frank Dawson.

I have always known that it would be virtually impossible for one person to write the story of Operation Raleigh: it's simply too big, and although I manage to visit most teams in the field, I don't get everywhere. Therefore in writing this book I have had to rely to a considerable extent on the work of members of

Central Headquarters and the expedition leaders themselves, many of whom kindly wrote a draft chapter for me. Nicky Poston's able assistance in producing the Peru chapter at short notice was especially appreciated. I am also deeply grateful to the dozens of Operation Raleigh organisers and Venturers who sent in contributions, some of which have been used; I hope to use others in follow-up books.

At the start I was ably assisted by Lisette Lecat, but she had to leave us suddenly due to a family bereavement, and I am eternally grateful to Blanche Debenham and Rowland Reeve, members of our volunteer staff, who kindly agreed to come aboard the flagship in Puerto Montt and work long hours at the Acorn Word Processors to produce this.

The photographs have been taken by many who risked themselves and their equipment on the expeditions, none more so than Chris Sainsbury. The selection of the photos has been made much easier thanks to the efforts of Operation Raleigh Promotions. Andrew Wright, the talented young artist who accompanied us for the first six months, has kindly drawn the splendid maps and sketches. Without Sue Farrington's efficiency in London and Peta Lock's help in the field, it would have been extremely difficult to amass all the material and I am also indebted to Operation Raleigh's agents, June Hall and Roger Schlesinger, for all their sound advice and encouragement.

This book is not just the story of the Venturers who came with us on the first fourteen months of Operation Raleigh, it is a tribute to all those who applied, many tens of thousands of them, who I know found the selection process itself challenging – I hope they have gone on to seek other endeavours. It can only tell part of the tale, but I pray it may encourage many more to follow those who have already sailed on the ships, and gone into the deserts, jungles, mountains and swamps, as Sir Walter Raleigh's colonists did when they went to the New World four hundred years ago.

John Blashford-Snell
Puerto Montt, Chile
January 1986

LIST OF SPONSORS

We would also like to express our gratitude to the following for making
Operation Raleigh possible.

A. W. SPOONER ESQ
ABBEY NATIONAL BUILDING
  SOCIETY
ABBOTT & BUTTERS LTD
ABBOTT LABORATORIES LTD
ABBOTTS PACKAGING
ABC TRAVEL GUIDES
ABC NEWS
ABELA MANAGEMENT SERVICES
  SA
ACORN COMPUTERS LTD
ACORN SOFTWARE LTD
ACTA PTY LTD
ACTION SPORTS
ACTT
ADAMSON–CHRONISTER VALVES
  INC
ADDIS LTD
ADDISON WESLEY PUBLISHING
AEI CABLES LTD
AEROPARTS ENGINEERING CO
  LTD
J. W. AGER & SONS LTD
AGFA GEVAERT LTD
AGIP STA
AIRCALL PLC
AIR FLORIDA (EUROPE)
AIR NEW ZEALAND UK
AIR PRODUCTS LTD
ALAN & SHEILA DIAMOND TRUST
ALAN COBHAM ENGINEERING
  LTD
ALBANY LIFE ASSURANCE
ALBERT BAXTER LTD
ALEXANDER DUCKHAM & CO LTD
ALICE (STANCOIL) LTD
ALLCORD LTD
A. & F. PEARS LTD
ALLEN & HANBURY LTD
ALLIANCE FREEZING CO
ALLIANCE FREEZING CO (SOUTH-
  LAND)
ALLIED CARPET STORES LTD
ALLIED FISHER SCIENTIFIC
ALLIED LYONS PLC
ALLIED MILLS
AMERICAN TOURISTER INC
A. M. HARRIS (P G) LTD
AMOCO UK LTD

AMOXIL BRAND EXECUTIVE
ANCHOR FOODS LTD
ANDREW CHALMERS & MITCHELL
  LTD
ANDREW WEIR & CO LTD
A. N. McKENZIE CHARITABLE
  TRUST
ANDREW JOHNSON KNUDSON
  LTD
ANDREW, CHALMERS &
  MITCHELL LTD
ANDREWS INDUSTRIAL
  EQUIPMENT LTD
ANFIELD FOUNDATION
ANGLIA CANNERS LTD
ANGLO-PERUVIAN SOCIETY
ANNENBERG FOUNDATION
ANSETT TRUST
ANTHONY HORNBY CHARITABLE
  TRUST
ANTHONY JAMES STUDIO
ANTLER LUGGAGE
ANTLER OF PALL MALL
ANTONY BOWRING ESQ
APOLLO INDUSTRIAL AND
  GENERAL
AQUAFINE (UK) LTD
AQUALAC (SPRING WATERS) LTD
AQUAMAN UK LTD
ARC GROUP
ARGOS DISTRIBUTORS
ARMCO FINANCIAL SERVICES
ARMITAGE SHANKS & CO LTD
ARMSTRONG MOTOR CYCLES LTD
ARMSTRONG PATENTS CO LTD
ARMOUR PHARMACEUTICAL CO
ARNETTS BAKERY
ARNOLD ZIEF ESQ
ARNOLD LAVER & CO LTD
ARTFLOW STUDIOS
ARTHUR GUINNESS & SONS PLC
ARTIST HOME SUPPLIES
ARUN PRODUCTS LTD
ASC
ASLAND WORLDWIDE INC
ASSOCIATED BRITISH FOODS PLC
ASSOCIATED BRITISH PORTS
ASSOCIATED CONTAINER TRANS-
  PORT EASTOP (AUSTRALIA) LTD

ASSOCIATED FISHERIES
ASSOCIATED LEAD MANU-
  FACTURERS
ASSOCIATED STEAMSHIP AGENCY
A. T. & B. BARNARD
ARCO
ATHENA PRODUCTIONS
ATKINSON AND PRICKETT LTD
ATLAS COPCO (GB) LTD
AUDIO DESIGN CALREC LTD
AUDIO VISUAL EDUCATIONAL
  SYSTEMS CO
AURORA PLC
AUSTRALIAN CITY PROPERTIES
J. W. AUTOMARINE
AUTOMATED MARINE PRO-
  PULSION
AVM FERROGRAPH
AVON INFLATABLES LTD
AVON RUBBER PLC
AWDRY, WYLES & BAILEY
A. W. GALE CHARITABLE TRUST
H. AYTON ESQ

B. A. BEADLE & CO LTD
B. H. GASKELL ESQ
B. J. MANNING ESQ
BBC PUBLICATIONS
B. COOKE & SON LTD
BAII (BANQUE ARABE)
BAHAMAS WELDINGS FIRE
BALTIC EXCHANGE
BANK OF SCOTLAND
BANTEX STATIONERY LTD
BP CHEMICALS LTD
BARD'S SMOKED SALMON LTD
BARNEY'S PR
BARCLAYS BANK PLC
BARCLAYCARD CHIEF OFFICE
BARCLAYS LIFE ASSURANCE CO
  LTD
BARNARDOS DISTRIBUTION
BARNES & MULLINS LTD
BART SPICES
BARTLETT CHEMICALS INC
BASIL SHIPPAM CHARITABLE
  TRUST
BASKETMAKERS COMPANY
BASS EXPORT LTD

BASS PLC
BATCHELORS FOODS LTD
BATLEY GS PARENTS ASSOCI-
ATION
BAUSCH & LOMB UK LTD
BEATRICE LAING TRUST
BEAUCHAMP CRADICK
ASSOCIATES
BEAVERBROOK FOUNDATION
B. E. GREEN ESQ
BEECHAM RESEARCH LABORA-
TORIES
BELLWAY MARINE
BELLWAY PLC
BENDER & CASSEL LTD
BENHAM CHARITABLE SETTLE-
MENT
BENNS INFORMATION SERVICES
BERGEN & BALL
BERGHAUS LTD
BERNARD PIGGOTT TRUST
BERNARD SUNLEY FOUNDATION
BEROL LTD
BESCO BARON LTD
BICC
BILL MOORE PRODUCTS
BILLINGSGATE TRADERS LTD
BINATONE INTERNATIONAL LTD
BIRDS EYE WALLS LTD
BIRKBECK MONTAGU
BLACKBURN RURAL INDUSTRIES
BLACK & DECKER
BLACK & EDGINGTON HIRE LTD
BLACKBURNS ALUMINIUM LTD
BLAIR ADAM HOUSE
BLAKE & SONS (GOSPORT) LTD
BLACK 'N' WHITE
BLUE CIRCLE INDUSTRIES PLC
BLUNDELL PERMOGLAZE LTD
BOB RAYSON ESQ
BOEHRINGER CORP LONDON LTD
BOEHRINGER INGELHEIM LTD
BOOTS COMPANY LTD
BOSTIC LTD
BOURNVILLE WORKS CHARI-
TABLE CO LTD
BOVRIL LTD
BOWATER SCOTT CORPORATION
PLC
BOWRING CHARITIES
FOUNDATION
BOWYERS WILTSHIRE LTD
BOYD STEAMSHIP CORPORATION
BP CHEMICALS LTD (HULL)
BPCC DESIGN & PRINT LTD
BRAITHWAITE BULLOCK & CO
LTD
BREWERS COMPANY
BRIGADIER H. R. W. VERNON
BRISTOL UNIFORMS LTD
BRITISH ARKADY CO LTD
BRITISH ASSOC IND EDITORS
LTD
BRITANNIA ARROW HOLDINGS PLC

BRITISH AEROSPACE
BRITISH AIRWAYS
BRITISH ALCAN ALUMINIUM
LTD
BRITISH AMERICAN OPTICAL CO
LTD
BRITISH AMERICAN TOBACCO CO
BRITISH BROADCASTING
CORPORATION
BRITISH CALEDONIAN AIRWAYS
BRITISH CENTRAL ELECTRICITY
CO LTD
BRITISH FISH CANNERS (FRASER-
BURGH) LTD
BRITISH GAS
BRITISH MICO
BRITISH NATIONAL INSURANCE
CO LTD
BRITISH NATIONAL LIFE
ASSURANCE CO
BRITISH NUCLEAR FUELS LTD
BRITISH OLIVETTI LIMITED
BRITISH OXYGEN CHEMICALS
LTD
BRITISH RAIL
BRITISH RED CROSS SOCIETY
BRITISH ROAD SERVICES
(SOUTHERN)
BRITISH SALT LTD
BRITISH SHIP BUILDERS
BRITISH STEEL CORPORATION
BRITISH SUB AQUA CLUB
BRITISH TELECOM CENTRE
BRITISH TELECOM INTER-
NATIONAL
BRITISH VINEGARS LTD
BRITOIL PLC
BRITVIC LTD
BRIXTON ESTATE PLC
BROTHER INDUSTRIES LTD
BRYANT BROADCAST & DATA
COMMS
BSC PLATES
BUCKLAND PRESS GROUP LTD
BUDGET CARS
BUDGET RENT-A-CAR
BUITONI CATERING PRODUCTS
BURMAH CATERING PRODUCTS
BURMAH CASTROL LTD
BURTON CHARITABLE TRUST
BUTLINS PLC
BUTTER DANE UK LTD

C. & A. ROCKES CHARITABLE
TRUST
C. B. NORTH LTD
C. & J. CLARKE LTD
C. T. BOWRING LTD
C. B. NORTH LTD
C. D. STARTIN
C. SHIPPHAMS & CO
CADBURY SCHWEPPES
(AUSTRALIA)
CADBURY SCHWEPPES (ENGLAND)

CADOGAN TATE LTD
CALDBECK INTERNATIONAL LTD
CALOR GAS LTD
CALOUSTE GULBENKIAN
FOUNDATION
CAMBERWELL SCHOOL OF ARTS
AND CRAFTS
CAMBRIDGE TUTORS EDUCA-
TIONAL TRUST
CANADA DRY RAWLINGS LTD
CANNON INDUSTRIES LTD
CANON UK LTD
CAPE BOARDS & PANELS LTD
CAPPER PASS & SON LTD
CAPE INDUSTRIES PLC
CAPPS QUICK PRINT
CARAVAN CLUB
CARAVEL MANUFACTURING LTD
CARIBBEAN PAINT MANU-
FACTURING CO LTD
CARLSBERG BREWERIES LTD
CARNATION FOODS CO LTD
CARNEGIE DUNFERMLINE TRUST
CAROLINA SKIFF INC
CARPENTERS SHIPPING
CARSTON ELECTRONICS LTD
CARTWRIGHT & BUTLER
CASELLA LONDON LTD
CASSENE
CASTLE & COOKE FOOD SALES
CO LTD
CASTLE HILL HOSPITAL
CANADIAN PACIFIC AIR LINES
CAVE FOUNDATION
CEE VEE ENGINEERING LTD
CENTRAL ELECTRICITY
GENERATING BOARD
CENTRONIC DATA COMPUTERS
(UK) LTD
CENTRONIC LTD
CETA PRINT
CETA PROCESSING
CHAMBERS & FARGUS
CHAPMAN ENVELOPES
CHASE MANHATTEN BANK
CHAS. F. THACKRAY LTD
CHATSWORTH LTD
CHAUCER FOODS LTD
CHEVRON OVERSEAS PETROLEUM
LTD
CHILETABACOS
CHILTERN FOODS LTD
CHLORIDE EUROPE
CHLORIDE MOTIVE POWER
CHLORIDE STANDBY SYSTEMS
CHRISTIAN SALVESEN (COLD
STORAGE) LTD
CHRISTIES LTD
CHRISTINE PROTCHARD
CHRISTOPHER LAING FOUNDA-
TION
CHUBB FIRE SECURITY LTD
CHUBB LOCK CO
CINE EUROPE LTD

CITIBANK
CITICORP INSURANCE BROKERS
    LTD
CITY OF PLYMOUTH
CLARK INDUSTRIES LTD
CLEGHORN WARING & CO
    (PUMPS) LTD
CLENGLASS ELECTRIC LTD
CLINICAL SOCIETY OF BATH
CLINIQUE LABORATORIES LTD
CLOTHWORKERS FOUNDATION
COALITE GROUP PLC
COATES & CO (PLYMOUTH) LTD
COOPER ARV
COOPERS & LYBRAND
CO-OPERATIVE WHOLESALE LTD
COLEMAN (UK) INC
COLIN JAMES ESQ
COLIN MACADIE ESQ
COLMANS OF NORWICH
COLOUR PROCESSING LABS LTD
COMET GROUP PLC
COMPAGNIE GENERAL MARITIME
COMMERCIAL CONTAINER TRANS-
    PORT LTD
COMPAIR INDUSTRIAL LTD
COMPAIR REAVELL LTD
COMPASS MARITIME
COMPUTER CONCEPTS
CONOCO (UK) LTD
CONSERVATIVE CENTRAL OFFICE
CONSOLIDATED GOLD FIELDS
CONTINENTAL GRAIN CO
COPE ALLMAN PLASTICS LTD
CORK BAYS & FISHER LTD
CORNWALL MINING SERVICES
COSTAIN PROCESS LTD
COTSWOLD CAMPING
COUNTESS GRETA BERNARD
COURTAULDS PLC
COVENTRY BUILDING SOCIETY
CPC (UK) LTD
CRANE PACKAGING LTD
CRAYONNE LTD
C. R. M. BUCHANAN
CRYPTO PEERLESS LTD
CULPEPPER LTD
CUMMINS ENGINE CO LTD
CUNARD BROCKLEBANK
CYB LTD

DAIRY CREST FOODS
D. A. MACRAE LTD
DAILY TELEGRAPH
DALGETY PLC
DANARM LTD
B. DANBY & CO LTD
DANIEL J. EDELMAN LTD
DARTINGTON FARM FOODS LTD
DASHWOOD BREWER & PHILIPPS
    LTD
DAVID AUSTIN ROSES
DAVID ESSEX ESQ
DAVID PINDER & PARTNERS

DAVY & CO (LONDON) LTD
DAWNFRESH SEAFOODS LTD
DCL FOOD GROUP
DDD (SECURITY SYSTEMS) LTD
DEAK & CO INC
DEAN & CHAPTER OF WESTMINSTER
DEB CHEMICAL PROPRIETARIES
    LTD
DECCA RADAR LTD
DELMAR CHARITABLE TRUST
DELOITTE HASKINS & SELLS
DENCO LTD
DELTA AIRLINES
DENTSU INC
DENTSPLY LTD
DEPT OF EDUCATION & SCIENCE
DEXION LTD
DHL INTERNATIONAL (UK) LTD
DIVEMEX LTD
D. J. CRESSWELL ESQ
J. & M. DOLMETSCH LTD
DONALD BROWN (BROWNALL) LTD
DONALD STEVENSON
DONCASTER DEPUTISING SERVICE
DOUGLAS MARTIN TRUST
DOROTHY HOLMES CHARITABLE
    TRUST
DOWLINGS SEWING MACHINES LTD
DOWSETT ENGINEERING CON-
    STRUCTION LTD
DR L. H. A. PILKINGTONS
    CHARITABLE SETTLEMENT
DRAEGER SAFETY LTD
DUDLEY COX CHARITABLE TRUST
DUDLEY JEHAN
DULVERTON TRUST
DUNLOP INDUSTRIAL &
    PROTECTIVE
DUNLOP MARINE SAFETY
    PRODUCTS
DURAPIPE LTD
DYLON INTERNATIONAL LTD

E. A. SMITH ESQ
E. D. CADBURY CHARITABLE TRUST
E. M. RIORDAN ESQ
E. P. BARRUS LTD
E. LEITZ INSTRUMENTS LTD
EDEN VALE
EDUCATIONAL MAILING SERVICES
EGA LTD
ECHO-TOOL
EAST RIDING FARM PRODUCTS LTD
EASTERBROOK ALLCARD & CO LTD
EDELRID (UK) LTD
EDDYSTONE RADIO LTD
EDWARD STAMFORD LTD
ELBAR-PINEFIELD LTD
ELECTRICITY COUNCIL
ELECTRO FURNACE PRODUCTS LTD
ELECTROLUX LTD
ELEY IMPERIAL METALS
    INDUSTRIES LTD
ELLIS BOOKER LTD

ELLINGER, HEATH, WESTERN & CO
EMTRAD LTD
ENSIGN FLAG CO LTD
ENVIRODOOR MARKUS LTD
ERIC E. HOTUNG ESQ
EQUITY & LAW CHARITY
ERCOL FURNITURE LTD
ERNST & WHINNEY
ESCHMANN BROTHERS & WALSH
    LTD
ESSELTE LETRASET
ETHICON
EUROPOWER HYDRAULICS LTD
EVER READY LTD
EXPRESS DAIRIES
EXTON & GOLD LTD

F. E. WRIGHT (UK) LTD
F. J. PARSONS & CO LTD
FABER PREST HOLDINGS PLC
FAIRCLOUGH BUILDINGS LTD
FARLEYS HEALTH PRODUCTS LTD
SIR HENRY FARRINGTON BT
FENWICK LTD
H. FINE & SON LTD
FINDLATER MAKIE TODD & CO
    LTD
FISCO PRODUCTS
FISHMONGERS COMPANY
FISONS CHARITABLE TRUST
FITZMAURICE HOUSE LTD
FLAG TRAVEL LTD
FLYING TIGERS
FOOD BROKERS LTD
FOOTWEAR LTD
FORBO UK LTD
FORD MOTOR CO LTD
FOX'S BISCUITS
FORESTRALL LTD
FOULDS & SONS
FOUNTAIN DRINKS
FOUNTAINHEAD PUBLICITY &
    ADVERTISING
F. R. SCOTT LTD
FRANK W. JOEL LTD
FRANKFURTER ALLGEMEINE
FREDERICK OLIVER LTD
FREEPORT ADVERTISING AND
    PRINTING LTD
FREEPORT GASES LTD
FREEPORT HARBOUR CO LTD
FRONTLINE VIDEO FACILITIES LTD
FROZEN QUALITY LTD
FUJI PHOTO FILM (UK) LTD
FURNESS WITHEY (SHIPPING) LTD

G. C. COOPER ESQ
G. K. MATHEWS & ASSOCIATES LTD
G. S. PLAUT CHARITABLE TRUST
GALLAGHER LTD
GALLENKAMP & CO LTD
G. & A. E. SLINGSBY LTD
G. M. MORRISON CHARITABLE
    TRUST

LIST OF SPONSORS

G. & M. POWER PLANT & CO
G. S. VOASE LTD
G. W. BIGGS & SONS LTD
G. W. LATUS
G. W. SPARROW & SONS
GANDARA PANAMA SA
GARUDA INDONESIAN AIRLINES
GAS & EQUIPMENT LTD
GATEWAY FOODMARKETS LTD
GAULT R DEVELOPMENTS LTD
GEIMUPLAST
GEORGE DREXLER OFREX
　FOUNDATION
GEORGE HAMMOND LTD
GEORGE WIMPEY & CO LTD
GENESIS PR LTD
GEORGE PHILIP & SON
GEOGRAPHICAL MAGAZINE
GERRARD INDUSTRIES LTD
GESTETNER HOLDINGS PLC
GESTETNER INTERNATIONAL LTD
GESTETNER UK LTD
GILMAN & CO LTD
GLAXO LABORATORIES LTD
GLEN REELS LTD
GLOBE ENGINEERING LTD
GODINGTON CHARITABLE TRUST
GOLD CROSS PHARMACEUTICALS
GOLDEN ARROW MACHINE
GOLDEN WONDER PLC
GOODYEAR TYRE & RUBBER CO
GOODYEAR PACKAGING
GOURMET FROZEN FOODS EXPORT
　CO
GRAHAM POULTER PUBLIC
　RELATIONS
GRAHAM YOUNG ESQ
GRANADA FOUNDATION
GRAND BAHAMA BAKERY LTD
GRAND METROPOLITAN GROUP
GRAND METROPOLITAN HOTELS
GRANET COMMUNICATIONS LTD
GREAT BRITAIN SASAKAWA
　FOUNDATION
GREENHAM TRADING LTD
GREIG, MIDDLETON & COMPANY
GROSVENOR ESTATES
GROUP III INC
GROVES, W. H. & FAMILY LTD
G. T. MANAGEMENT
GUENOC WINERY
GUEST, KEEN & NETTLEFOLDS PLC
GUINNESS PEAT GROUP PLC
GUNTER CHARITABLE TRUST

H. P. BULMERS LTD
H. CLARKSON & CO LTD
H. E. REYNOLDS
H. & T. MARLOW LTD
H. J. HEINZ & CO LTD
HMS RALEIGH
HM STRATFORD
HALDANE FOODS LTD
HALIFAX BUILDING SOCIETY

HALLEYS COMET SOCIETY
HALL'S BARTON ROPERY CO LTD
HALL & WOODHOUSE LTD
HALTRAC LTD
HAMMERSMITH & FULHAM
　COUNCIL
HAMPTON SCHOOL
HANSCO LTD
HANDLEY, W. A. CHARITY TRUST
HANY SALAAM
HARLANDS OF HULL LTD
HARRISON COWLEY PUBLIC
　RELATIONS
HARRODS LTD
HAWLEY GROUP PLC
HAX LTD
HAZLEWOOD FOODS PLC
HEATOVENT ELECTRIC LTD
HEDGES & BUTLER
HELIX LTD
HEMPEL'S MARINE PRINTS LTD
HENRI-LLOYD LTD
HENDRY BROTHERS (LONDON) LTD
HENSMAN
HERBERT SLATER LTD
HERBERT SMITH & CO LTD
HERON CORPORATION
HERON POWER PRODUCTS LTD
HEYGATES LTD
HIATT & COMPANY
HICKSON'S TIMBER PRODUCTS LTD
HIGHLAND SPRING LTD
HILTON COLOUR LTD
HOARE GOVETT
HODGE SEPARATORS LTD
HOGG, ROBINSON CARGO LTD
HOGG ROBINSON CHARITABLE
　TRUST
HOGG ROBINSON TRAVEL LTD
HOLIDAY INN
HOLMES TANNERS LTD
HOME DEPOT
HONEYWELL LTD
HONG KONG BANK FOUNDATION
HP FOODS LTD
H. P. BULMER LTD
HUBBARD-READER GROUP LTD
HULL CITY AFC PLC
HULL CITY COUNCIL
HULL FISHING VESSEL OWNERS
HULL TELEPHONE CO
HUMBER FREEZER TRAWLER
　OWNERS CO LTD
HUMBERSIDE WELDING SUPPLIES
HUNTING GROUP
HUNTLY & PALMER FOODS LTD
HUTTON & CO (SHIPS CHANDLERS)
　LTD
HYETT ADAMS LTD

IAN MACKENSON-SANDBACK ESQ
IAN REEVES ESQ
I. D. FRASER
IBERIA INTERNATIONAL AIRWAYS

IBM UK LTD
IBSONMAIN LTD
ICE 'N' EASY SEAFOODS
ICI LTD
ICI VISIQUEEN POLYTHENE FILM
　PRODS
IDEAL STANDARD LTD
IDLEWILD TRUST
IMPALLOY LTD
IMPERIAL BREWING AND LESIURE
　LTD
IMPERIAL BUSINESS EQUIPMENT
IMPERIAL CHEMICAL INDUSTRIES
IMPERIAL LIFE ASSURANCE CO OF
　CANADA
IMPERIAL PROFESSIONAL COATING
INFORMATION SERVICES LTD
INSTITUTE OF MARKETING
INTERCONTINENTAL HOTELS
INTERNATIONAL DISTILLERS
　VINTNERS (UK) LTD
INTERNATIONAL LABS LTD
INTERNATIONAL SIGNAL AND
　CONTROL GROUP PLC
INVERESK
ITT CONSUMER PRODUCTS UK LTD
ITT JABSCO LTD
IVOR INNES PHOTOGRAPHY
ITV

J. A. DUTTON ESQ
J. A. MARSHALL & CO (SOUTHERN)
　LTD
J. D. POTTER LTD
J. GRESHAM & CO LTD
J. KNAGGS & CO LTD
J. H. FENNER AND CO LTD
J. MARR & SON LTD
J. MEREDITH BUSINESS EQUIPMENT
J. MOSELEY ESQ
J. R. LAXTON ESQ
J. R. DUGARD ESQ
J. S. MILSON ESQ
J. LYONS & COMPANY LTD
J. J. VICKERS & SONS
J. M. K. LAING FOUNDATION
J. POORE ESQ
J. S. POSGATE ESQ
J. W. AGER & SONS LTD
J. T. SCOTWAY LTD
J. YOULE & CO LTD
JACOBS
JACOS & PARTNERS
JAEGER HOLDINGS LTD
JAGUAR CARS LTD
JAMES BOWMAN & SONS
JAMES BURROUGH PLC
JAMES, FREDERICK & ETHEL ANNE
　MEASURES CHARITY
JAMES HAMILTON LTD
JANES DEFENCE WEEKLY
JANE HODGE FOUNDATION
JAMES MOGGRIDGE WINES
JANSSEN PHARMACEUTICAL LTD

JAPAN AIR LINES CO LTD
JARDINE GLANVILLE INSURANCE
  BROKERS
JAVERETTE
JAYBEAM LIMITED
JEBSON & CO LTD
JENKS BROKERAGE
JESSOPS OF LEICESTER LTD
JOE BROWN SHOP
JOHN BULL LTD
JOHN BURGESS & SON LTD
JOHN & JANE NORTON
JOHN F. CORLYON (FURNITURE)
  LTD
JOHN FINLAN PLC
JOHN PLUMER & PARTNERS LTD
JOHN REID ESQ
JOHN RIDGEWAY SCHOOL OF
  ADVENTURE
JOHN SMITH CBE JP DL
JOHN TAWS LTD
JOHN TRELAWNEY LTD
JOHN WEST FOODS LIMITED
JOHNSON WAX LTD
JOHNSONS OF HENDON LTD
JOHN WRIGHT & SONS
JOHNSON & JOHNSON
JOHNSTON'S CONSTRUCTION
  COMPANY
JONES & BROTHER LTD
N. G. JOSEPH ESQ
JOSEPH WALKER
JULIANAS DISCOTHEQUES
JUSTERINI & BROOKS LTD

KARRIMOR INTERNATIONAL LTD
KATIE FENWICK
KAY & CO LTD
KHD GREAT BRITAIN LTD
K SHOEMAKERS LTD
KEELERS LTD
KEITH TOPHAM ESQ
KELVIN HUGHES CHARTS &
  MARITIME SUPPLIES LTD
KEMPNER CORPORATION
KENCO COFFEE CO LTD
KENCO TYPHOO CATERING
  SERVICES
KENNETH WILSON HOLDINGS LTD
KENREY ELECTRONICS LTD
KERR STEAMSHIP CO INC
KILLGERM CHEMICALS LTD
KING TOUR JG
KINGS TOWN ENGRAVING CO LTD
KIRBY LAING FOUNDATION
KLARK-TEKNIK
KLEINWORT BENSON (TRUSTEES)
  LTD
KNOWLEDGE-INDEX
KODAK LTD
KROY (EUROPE) LTD
KRUPP ATLAS ELEKTRONIK UK
  LTD
K. W. DALE OBE TD CENG RCIBS

LBC
L. C. GRAINGER ESQ
L. E. F. BISHOP LTD
L. E. PRITCHITT & CO LTD
L. E. WEST & CO LTD
LADY SHEILA BUTLIN
LAING INDUSTRIAL ENGINEERING
  & CONSTRUCTION LTD
LAINGS CHARITABLE TRUST
LANDORE METAL PRODUCTS
LANDSDOWNE CLUB
LAND ROVER LTD
LANE FOX & PARTNERS
LANSING BAGNALL LTD
LAZARD BROS
LEA & PERRINS LTD
LEAFE & HAWKES (CHARTERING)
  LTD
LEDERLE LABORATORIES
LEE COOPER GROUP PLC
LEEDS & HOLBECK BUILDING
  SOCIETY
LEE HYSAN ESTATE CO LTD
LEGAL & GENERAL GROUP PLC
LEOPOLD DE ROTHSCHILD TRUST
LEROCO EXPORTS LTD
LESLIE & GODWIN CHARITABLE
  TRUST
LETRASET
LEVER BROS LTD
LEX SERVICES PLC
LEYLAND PAINT & WALLPAPER PLC
LIFEGUARD EQUIPMENT LTD
LIGHT ALLOY LTD
LINC INTERNATIONAL COM-
  MUNICATIONS
LION FOODS LTD
LIPHA PHARMACEUTICALS LTD
LIPTON EXPORT LTD
LIQABUE PANAMA
LITTLE SHIP CLUB
LITTLEMORE SCIENTIFIC
  ENGINEERING
LLANDOR METAL PRODUCTS
LLOYDS BANK PLC
LLOYDS CHARITIES TRUST
LLOYD'S REGISTER OF SHIPPING
LLOYDS OF LONDON PRESS LTD
LOCKWOODS
LOFTHOUSE OF FLEETWOOD LTD
LOIE G. HACKING ESQ
LOM FOOD SERVICES
LONDONS SCOTTISH MARINE OIL
  PLC
LONDON CHAMBER OF COMMERCE
LONDON LAW TRUST
LONDON SCOTTISH
LONDON WINDSURFING CENTRE
LONDON UNDERGROUND LTD
LONRHO PLC
LORD COZEN-HARDY'S NIMROD
  AND GLAVEN MACFARLANES
  TRUST
LORD VESTEY

LUCY JANE THOMPSON
LYON EQUIPMENT

MAP
M. E. G. MOORE LTD
MEL LTD
M. G. DUFF MARINE LTD
M. H. FISHER
M. HARLAND & SONS LTD
MAERSK CO LTD
MAGDALEN HOSPITAL TRUST
MAJOR GENERAL SIR GERLAD DUKE
MAJOR E. TEMPLE
MAJOR P. ROBINSON
MALAYSAIN AIRLINE SYSTEM
MALCOLM WEST PLANT HIRE LTD
MALLINSON DENNY LTD
MANDARIN HOTEL, JAKARTA
MANLEY RATCLIFFE LTD
MANPOWER (HUMBER) WORK
  CONTRACTORS
MANPOWER SERVICES COMMISSION
MANNESMANN TALLY LTD
MARCONI INTERNATIONAL MARINE
  CO LTD
MARCONI RADAR SYSTEMS LTD
MARCONI SECURE RADIO SYSTEMS
  LTD
MARCONI SPACE DEFENCE SYSTEMS
MARFLEET REFINING CO LTD
MARINE POWER INTERNATIONAL
MARINE PROJECTS (PLYMOUTH)
MARINE SOCIETY
MARK C. BROWN & SON LTD
MARK PRODUCING COMPANY INC
MATTHEW GLOAG & SON LTD
MARLBOROUGH COMMUNICATIONS
  LTD
MARS CONFECTIONARY LTD
MARTINDALE PROTECTION LTD
MATTHEW HALL ENGINEERING
  LTD
MATTHEWS BUTCHERS LTD
MAUD ELKINGTON CHARITABLE
  TRUST
MAY & BAKER LTD
MAYFIELD BROS LTD
McCAIN INTERNATIONAL LTD
McCANN-ERICKSON
McKELLER WATTS
MEAT PROMOTION EXECUTIVE
MELBA TRADING CO LTD
MELSON WINGATE LTD
MENDHAM ENGINEERS LTD
MEPR MICRODATA SYSTEMS LTD
MERCERS LIVERY COMPANY
MERCHANT TAYLOR'S SCHOOL
MERRYDOWN WINE PLC
MERSEY FREIGHT SERVICE
MERSEYSIDE COUNTY COUNCIL
MESSRS WILLIAM CHARLES
  CROCKER
METAL BOX PLC (HULL) LTD
METROPOLITAN POLICE OFFICE

MICROVITEC PLC
MICHAEL RHYS JENKINS ESQ
MIDDLESEX RFU MEMORIAL TRUST
MIDLAND & SCOTTISH MARINE
  INVESTMENT CO LTD
MIDSHIP MARINE INC
MIKE PAGE OFFICE SUPPLIES
MIMAC
MIMS
MINIGRIP (LONDON) LTD
MIRACLE TECHNOLOGY (UK) LTD
M. K. ELECTRIC LTD
MOBIL OIL CO
MOET & CHANDON
MOLYSLIP HOLDINGS LTD
MONO PUMPS LTD
MONTAGUE L. MEYER (HULL) LTD
MOODY FOUNDATION
MOORE PARAGON UK LTD
MOORE STREET MANAGEMENT
MOORES AND ROWLAND
MORANE PLASTIC CO LTD
MORGAN CRUCIBLE COMPANY
  FUND
MORGAN GRENFELL & CO LTD
MORNING FOODS LTD
MOTOROLA INC
MOY-PARK LTD
MR & MRS C. JONES
MR AND MRS J. A. PAYNE'S CHARITY
MR GRAVES
MRS A. EARLE
MRS C. P. NOEL
MRS E. NOBLE
MRS LYNDA THOMPSON
MRS M. M. GILL CHARITABLE
  TRUST
MRS V. S. STANHOPE-PALMERS
  CHARITY
MRS M. CORNES
MULTILINK
3M (UK) PLC

NAIRN FLOORS LTD
NABISCO BRANDS LTD
NATIONAL CAR PARKS LTD
NATIONAL COAL BOARD (SOUTH
  MIDLANDS)
NATIONAL COAL BOARD (NORTH
  NOTTINGHAM)
NATIONAL SAVINGS BANK
NATIONAL WESTMINSTER BANK
NATIONWIDE BUILDING SOCIETY
NEEDLERS PLC
NEILL TOOLS LTD
NESTLE CO LTD
NESTLES CORPORATION USA
NETLON LTD
NEWCASTLE UPON TYNE COUNCIL
  FOR VOLUNTARY SERVICE
NEW CHESHIRE SALT WORKS LTD
NEW STRAITS TIMES
NEWS GROUP NEWSPAPER LTD
NEW ZEALAND MEAT PROMOTIONS

NEWAGE ENGINEERS LTD
NICHOLAS LABORATORIES LTD
NIGEL GIFFORD LTD
NIPPONDENSO CO LTD
NORDIA
NORMAN FAMILY CHARITABLE
  TRUST
NORMAN WALKER (MACHINERY)
  LTD
NORTECH SERVICES LTD
NORTH BRITISH MARINE GROUP
  LTD
NORTH FACE (SCOTLAND) LTD
NORTH SEA MEDICAL CENTRE
NORTH STAFF & SOUTH CHESHIRE
  BROADCASTING LTD
NORTHERN FOODS LTD
NORTHERN ROCK BUILDING
  SOCIETY
NORTHERN SINK SUPPLIES LTD
NORTHWOOD COLOUR CENTRE LTD

OCE COPIERS
OCCIDENTAL INTERNATIONAL OIL
  INC
OCEAN PUBLICATIONS
OFFICE & ELECTRONIC MACHINES
  LTD
OLDHAM BATTERIES LTD
OPTICAL & TEXTILE LTD
OPTREX LTD
ORION INSURANCE
OSRAM (GEC)
OVERSEAS COMMODITIES LTD
OVERSEAS CONTAINERS LTD
OVERSEAS TRADING CORPORATION
OZALID UK LTD

P. A. LUCAS ESQ
PEC PHOTOGRAPHIC ELECTRICAL
  CO LTD
PETER DE SAVARAY ESQ
P. D. PLASTICS LTD
P. F. CHARITABLE TRUST
P. H. POND-JONES
P. M. PARTNERSHIP
P. WILLOUGHBY LTD
PACIFIC STEAM NAVIGATION CO
PADDINGTON CHARITABLE
  ESTATES
PAINS WESSEX SCHEMULY LTD
PAN AMERICAN WORLD AIRWAYS
PANAMA MARINE SAFETY AND
  SUPPLY
PANASONIC TECHNICS UK LTD
PARK ADVERTISING MARKETING
PARKE DAVIS RESEARCH
  LABORATORIES
PARSONS BROTHERS LTD
PARTORIA ENGINEERING LTD
PASTA FOODS LTD
PATRICIA OAKLEY
PATERSON PRODUCTS LTD
PATAY PUMPS

PAULINE WAGNER
PEERLESS PLASTICS PACKAGING
PELLING AND CROSS LTD
PELTZ FOOD CORP
PERKINS ENGINES LTD
PEROLIN CO LTD
PERSTORP WARERITE LTD
PETER BLOOMFIELD CO LTD
PETER STERRY ESQ
PHAROS MARINE LTD
PHILIPS ELECTRONICS LTD
PHONOTAS GROUP LTD
PHOTOGRAPHIC ELECTRICAL CO
  LTD
PHYLISS ANGLISS
PILKINGTON BROS LTD
PITNEY BOWES PLC
PLESSEY MILITARY COMMUNI-
  CATIONS
POGO PRODUCING CO
POLYTECHNIC MARINE
PORTER BROTHERS
PORTH 84 LTD
POST OFFICE
POTTER CLARKE LTD
POWER TOOL HIRE
POWERSPORT INTERNATIONAL LTD
PRENTICE-HALL INTERNATIONAL
PRESTIGE GROUP LTD
PRIESTMAN BROS LTD
PRIMECUT FOODS LTD
L. E. PRITCHITT & CO LTD
PROCESS CONTROL CO
PROCTER & GAMBLE
PRODUCT SUPPORT GRAPHICS
PRUDENTIAL ASSURANCE CO LTD
PUNCH PUBLICATION LTD
PUSSERS NAVY RUM
PYE LTD
PYE TELECOMMUNICATIONS LTD
PYRAMID COMMUNICATIONS LTD
PYSER LTD

QANTAS AIRWAYS LTD
QUEENSWAY GROUP PLC

R. A. McKENNA ESQ
R. CURTISS AND SONS LTD
R. & E. COORDINATION LTD
R. S. COMPONENTS LTD
R. GAULT DEVELOPMENTS LTD
RABONE CHESTERMAN LTD
RACAL ACOUSTICS LTD
RACAL-DECCA MARINE
  NAVIGATION LTD
RACAL MARINE RADAR LTD
RACAL TACTICOM LTD
RADIATION TECHNOLOGY INC
RAINFORD TRUST
RANK FILM LABORATORIES LTD
RANK FOUNDATION
RANK HOVIS McDOUGALL LTD
RANK PULLIN CONTROLS
RANK XEROX (UK) LTD

RAPIDEX OF LONDON
RECKITT & COLEMAN (PHARMA-
  CEUTICALS)
RECKITT HOUSEHOLD
RECORD RIDGEWAY TOOLS LTD
REDIFFUSION CONSUMER
  ELECTRONICS LTD
REED CORRUGATED CASES LTD
REED INTERNATIONAL PLC
REED PUBLISHING LTD
REMPLOY
RENAULT UK LTD
RENTOKIL PRODUCTS DIVISION
RENTOKIL (SANITACT DIVISION)
REW
RFD GROUP PLC
RHM FOODS LTD
RICHARD CADBURY CHARITABLE
  TRUST
RICHARD DUNSTON (HESSLE) LTD
RICHARD JOHNSON & ASSOCIATES
RICHARD SIZER LTD
RICHMOND & RIGG PHOTOGRAPHY
RIDLEY INTERNATIONAL LTD
RIPLEY & CO LTD
ROBERT BRUCE FITZMAURICE LTD
ROBERTSON NESS TRUST
ROBIN CALDECOTE ESQ
ROBINSON HANNON LTD
ROCHE PRODUCTS LTD
R. S. DICKS ESQ
RON COOK ENGINEERING
ROSE & CO (HULL) LTD
ROSS FOODS LTD
ROTARY CLUB OF BINGLEY
ROTARY CLUB OF DROITWICH
ROTHSCHILD & SON, NH
ROTUNDA LTD
ROUSSEL LABORATORIES LTD
ROWAN-BENTALL CHARITY TRUST
ROWBOTHAM CHARITABLE TRUST
ROWNTREE MACKINTOSH PLC
ROYAL BANK OF CANADA
ROYAL BANK OF SCOTLAND PLC
ROYAL GEOGRAPHICAL SOCIETY
ROYAL JUBILEE TRUST
ROYAL NAVAL RESERVE OFFICERS
ROYALE PRINT LTD
ROYAL NEW ZEALAND NAVY
ROYAL SOVEREIGN LTD
ROYAL TRUST (CANADA)
RUSCADOR LTD
RUSSELL & McIVER LTD
RYCOTE MIC SHIELDS

SFD
SAATCHI & SAATCHI
SAGE FOODS
SALTER INDUSTRIAL MEASURE-
  MENT LTD
SAMUEL BANNER & CO LTD
SAMUELSON GROUP PLC
SAMUELSON LIGHTING LTD
SANTA FE (UK) LTD
SARGOM INTERNATIONAL LTD

SAVE & PROSPER EDUCATIONAL
  TRUST
SAVOY HOTELS PLC
SCAFLON LTD
SCHRODER CHARITABLE TRUST
SCHWARTZ SPICES LTD
SCOTFRESH LTD
SCUBAPRO (UK) LTD
SCOUTS (COUNTY OF GREATER
  LONDON NORTH)
SEA CONTAINERS LTD
SECOL LTD
SECURICOR LTD
SECURITY SERVICES PLC
SEDGEMOOR DISTRICT COUNCIL
SEFTON EXPLORATION ASSOCIATION
SEGAL & SONS LTD
SEIKO TIME
SELTEC AUTOMATION LTD
SERVIS DOMESTIC APPLIANCES LTD
SETON
SEVEN SEAS HEALTH CARE LTD
SHAW FOUNDATION
SHANDWICK PR CO LTD
SHELL EXPLORATION AND PRO-
  DUCTION (UK) LTD
SHELL TANKERS (UK) LTD
SHERWOOD MEDICAL INDUSTRIES
SHIPHAM & CO (PEGLERS)LTD
SHIPPING CORPS OF NEW ZEALAND
  (UK)
SHOEMAKERS LTD
SHORTS SPICES
SHOWERINGS LTD
SIEMENS LTD
SIGNS & LABELS LTD
SILVA (UK) LTD
SILVER REED UK LTD
SIR GEORGE MARTIN TRUST
SIR JACK HAYWARD KBE
SIR JULES THORN CHARITABLE
  TRUST
SIMON ROSEDOWNS LTD
SIMPSON LAWRENCE LTD
SIMPSON MARINE FRIDGES
  SYSTEMS
SIMPSON READY FOODS LTD
SKELLERUP INDUSTRIES
SKI WHIZZ
SMALL CRAFT DELIVERIES LTD
SMEDLEYS LTD
S. MCALLUM ESQ
SMITH & NEPHEW LTD
SMITH CHARITABLE TRUST
SMITHS INDUSTRIES LTD
SMYTHSON FRANK LTD
SNOWDEN MOULDING
SOCIETY OF MANUFACTURERS AND
  TRADERS
SOL TENCO LTD
SONY BROADCAST LTD
SONY MAGNETIC PRODUCTION
  DIVISION
SONY UK LTD
SOUTHERN PORT SERVICES

SOUTH MIDLANDS COMMUNI-
  CATIONS
SOUTHERN-EVANS (NUMBER) LTD
SPEAR & JACKSON TOOLS LTD
SPENDOR AUDIO SYSTEMS LTD
SPILLERS INTERNATIONAL LTD
SPOKESMAN COMMUNICATIONS
  LTD
SPRINGFIELD FIRE ARMS LTD
ST ANDREWS DOCK SURGERY
ST GEORGES DAY CLUB
ST MICHAELS MOUNT CHARITABLE
  FOUNDATION
ST IVEL LTD
ST JOHN AMBULANCE BRIGADE
STAEDTLER (UK) LTD
STANLEY TOOLS LTD
STARNA LTD
STELRAD GROUP LTD
STERLING HYDRAULICS LTD
STEVE JAMES & CO
STEWART WRIGHTSON CHARITY
  TRUST
STORNO LTD
STOTT AND SMITH GROUP LTD
STRUMECH ENGINEERING LTD
STRUTHERS & CARTER LTD
STUART LANIGAN ESQ
STUART PHARMACEUTICALS
STYLO PLC
SUB-SEA SERVICES
SUBSPEC
SUBSPEC INSPECTION CON-
  SULTANTS
SUE HAMMERSON CHARITABLE
  TRUST
SUN NEWSPAPER
SUPERFLIX LTD
SUPREME PLASTICS LTD
SUZUKI (GB) CARS LTD
SVENSKA ICI
SWINTEX LTD
SWISS BANK CORPORATION
SWS FILTRATION LTD SYSTEM
SYMINGTON'S

T. I. BRADBURY
T. I. RALEIGH INDUSTRIES
TANDBERG LTD
TANGANYIKA HOLDINGS
TANNOY LTD
TANQUERAY GORDON & CO
  LTD
TASCO SALES
TATE & LYLE PLC
TATTERSALLS LTD
TAYLOR WOODROW GROUP
TECHNOMATIC LTD
TELEDATA LTD
TELEX-VERLAG JAEGER AND
  WALDMANN GMBH UK BRANCH
TEMPCO UNION LTD
TENNECO EUROPE INC
TENNENT CALEDONIAN BREWERIES
TEXACO LTD

LIST OF SPONSORS

THE ANTHONY HORNBY CHARI-
TABLE TRUST
THE BANK LINE
THE BEDFORD CHARITY
THE BELIZE CONNECTION
THE BRITISH MARKET
THE CHAPMAN FOUNDATION
THE CIRIO CO LTD
THE DRAPERS CO
THE EMMOTT FOUNDATION LTD
THE FISH TRADER
THE GEORGE WIMPEY CHARITABLE
TRUST
THE GLOUCESTERSHIRE QUEENS
SILVER JUBILEE TRUST
THE GROCER
THE LIGHTHOUSE CLUB
THE LORD TAYLOR OF HADFIELD
THE MAERSK CO LTD
THE MANDARIN HOTEL JAKARTA
THE NEW COURT CHARITABLE
TRUST
THE READERS DIGEST
THE ROTHLEY TRUST
THE RYVITA CO LTD
THE SIR CYRIL KLEINWORT
CHARITABLE TRUST
THE TEA COUNCIL
THE WATES FOUNDATION
THETFORD MOULDED PRODUCTS
LTD
THOMAS & JAMES HARRISON LTD
THOMAS HILL ENGINEERING
(HULL) LTD
THOMAS HUDSON BENEVOLENT
TRUST
THOMAS MASON CHARITABLE
TRUST
THOMAS TUNNOCK LTD
THOMPSON MEDICAL CO
THOMPSON, LLOYD & EWART
THORN EMI LTD
THORN EMI VIDEO FACILITIES
THORN/EMI FERGUSON LTD
THORNGATE TRUST
TILDA RICE LTD
TIMES BOOKS
TIRFOR LTD
TOLLMAN-HUNDLEY HOTELS
TOME BEATTIE EDWARDS ESQ
TONY DUTTON ESQ
TOSHIBA (UK) LTD
TOWER HOTEL
TOWNE CEA (SHIP RIGGERS) LTD
TRADE AND TRAVEL PUBLICATIONS
T. R. DRAKE ESQ
TRANS AUSTRALIA AIRLINES
TRAVENOL LABORATORIES LTD
TREVOR AND BARRY MOSS
TRIATOM LTD
TROLL SAFETY EQUIPMENT LTD
TRUSTEE SAVINGS BANK
TSB CHANNEL ISLANDS
TSB LIFE LTD
TSB TRUST CO LTD

TUDOR TRUST
TULANE UNIVERSITY
TUPPERWARE CO
TUTOR SAFETY PRODUCTS LTD
TV/AVT
TVS
TWINNING CO LTD
TWO COUNTIES RADIO
T. W. POWELL ESQ
TWYDALE TURKEYS LTD
TYNE GANGWAY CO LTD
TYPOGRAPHICS LTD

UB (BISCUITS) LTD
ULSTER TELEVISION PLC
UNDERWATER INSTRUMENTATION
UNICORN CLUB
UNILEVER PLC
UNION INTERNATIONAL PLC
UNITED NEWSPAPERS LTD
UNITED SCIENTIFIC HOLDINGS
UNITOR SHIP SERVICE
UNWIN GRAIN LTD

VDU INSTALLATIONS LTD
V. W. PRODUCTS CHEMICALS
LTD
VALIN PRODUCTS
VAN LEER (UK) LTD
VANDENBURG ASSOCIATES
VANGO (SCOTLAND) LTD
VARIG BRAZILIAN AIRLINES
VDU INSTALLATIONS LTD
VECTOR INTERNATIONAL LTD
VERBATIM LTD
VIASA AIRWAYS
VICKERS PLC
VICKERS SHIPBUILDING & ENGIN-
EERING LTD
VIC RUDGE ESQ
VIDEOTEL MARINE INT LTD
VIEWPLAN LTD
VIKING LIFE SAVING EQUIPMENT
VINTNERS COMPANY
VIRGIN GROUP
VISCOUNT LEVERHULME
VOLKSWAGON MARKETING
VSEL

W. B. PHARMACEUTICALS LTD
W. H. GROVES & FAMILY LTD
W. H. SMITH & SON LTD
WACKER CHEMICALS LTD
WADDINGTON GAMES LTD
WALDMANN GMBH (UK)
WANDSWORTH COUNCIL
WALTER H. ANNENBERG KBE
WATER WEIGHTS
WCB MAILBOX LTD
WEDD DURLACHER MORDAUNT &
CO
WEDGEWOOD
WEEKS TRAILERS LTD
WELLCOME FOUNDATION
WELTON FOUNDATION

WELTONHURST LTD
WESTLAND PLC
WESTON HYDE PRODUCTS LTD
WESTMINSTER CHAMBER OF
COMMERCE
WESTMINSTER CITY COUNCIL
WHARTON WILLIAMS TAYLOR
WHATMAN LTD
WHEELS RENTALS LTD
WHITE'S ELECTRONICS (UK) LTD
WHITTINGHAM & PORTER LTD
WHITWORTHS HOLDINGS LTD
WIG & PEN CLUB
WIGGINS TEAPE GROUP LTD
WIGMORE MEDICAL EQUIPMENT
SUPPLIES
WILD HEERBRUGG (UK) LTD
WILFRID & CONSTANCE CAVE
FOUNDATION
WILKIN & SONS LTD
WILKINSON BROTHERS
WILKINSON SWORD LTD
WILLIAM BROADY & SON LTD
WILLIAM DAWSON PLC
WILLIAM GRANT & SONS
WILLIAM MALLINSON AND SONS
(SALES) LTD
WILLIAM PAGE CO LTD
WILLIAM PEARSON LTD
WILLIAMS AND GLYNS BANK
WILLIAMSON TEA HOLDINGS PLC
WILLS AND BATES LTD
WILLIS COMPUTER SUPPLIES LTD
WILSON'S OF SCOTLAND
WINCHESTER UK
WING TAT LEE ESQ
WOGEN ANNIVERSARY TRUST
WOODHOUSE DRAKE & CAREY LTD
WOOD'S TIMBER CO LTD
WORDPLEX LTD
WORLD TRADE CENTRE
WORSHIPFUL COMPANY OF
ACTUARIES
WORSHIPFUL COMPANY OF BAKERS
WORSHIPFUL COMPANY OF
BUTCHERS
WORSHIPFUL COMPANY OF
CHARTERED ACCOUNTANTS
WORSHIPFUL COMPANY OF
GARDENERS
WORSHIPFUL COMPANY OF
SHIPWRIGHTS

YMCA
YORKSHIRE DRY DOCK CO LTD
YORKSHIRE IMPERIAL FITTINGS
YORKSHIRE MARINE CONTAINERS
LTD
YORKSHIRE PLANT (HUMBER) LTD
YORKSHIRE POST
YORKSHIRE TV
YOULE & CO LTD

ZOELLNER & CO
ZONAL LTD